Tom & Bear

With great pleasure,
Richard McPhee

Best Wishes Tom and Bear

Tom & Bear

The Training of a Guide Dog Team

Text and photographs by Richard McPhee

Thomas Y. Crowell   New York

Library of Congress Cataloging in Publication Data
McPhee, Richard B.
Tom & Bear.
Summary: The author tells in diary format of his twenty-six days observing a young blind man training with a guide dog at Guiding Eyes for the Blind, a school in New York state.

1. Guide dogs—Training—Juvenile literature.
2. Kalec, Tom—Juvenile literature. 3. Guiding Eyes for the Blind, Inc.—Juvenile literature.
[1. Guide dogs—Training. 2. Blind]   I. Title.
HV1780.S4M35 1981   362.4'183   81-43031
AACR2
ISBN 0-690-04136-5
ISBN 0-690-04137-3 (lib. bdg.)

1 2 3 4 5 6 7 8 9 10
First Edition

For Tom and Bear

Joyce and Owen, Eileen and Indy, Caroline and Buffy, Anita and Sue, Sharon and Nolan, Dan and Tucker, Howard and Marty, Billy and Dolly, Joe and Tobias, Ross and Lance, Bob and Raft.

And for all guide dog teams everywhere. The staff of Guiding Eyes for the Blind, Inc. And all the trainers and instructors, breeders and kennel personnel, support staff, the 4-H families, the fundraisers and the volunteers and the fundgivers—for all who make it possible, God bless.

Contents

In this Rembrandt etching, blind Tobias is guided by a little dog.
Courtesy of Teylers Museum, Haarlem, The Netherlands

Introduction

For many years I have been full of questions about the guide dog teams that I've seen on the streets or on buses and in the subways. I have always been struck by the closeness and oneness of the relationship between blind people and their guide dogs. Obviously, it is a highly disciplined working relationship, and yet an extraordinarily gentle and loving one. How does it come about? How are guide dogs trained? How do blind people and guide dogs learn to work together safely as a team? Those are some of the questions that always came to mind.

A little more than a year ago, I finally managed to meet Geoff Lock, General Manager of Guiding Eyes for the Blind, Inc., in Yorktown Heights, New York, and Ted Zubrycki, Guiding Eyes' Director of Training. I explained to Geoff and Ted that as a writer and photographer I wanted to follow a young blind student, up close, through the twenty-six-day training program. After a second meeting, Geoff approved my idea and welcomed me to come live at Guiding Eyes "anytime I was ready."

It took almost a year to get ready and arrange enough time off from other work. And then the day I'd been waiting for came one Friday in June, and it came for many others as well. It came for Tom Kalec, a twenty-four-year-old blind diabetic from Columbia, South Carolina. It came for Bear, a nineteen-month-old golden retriever. And it came for eleven other students from all parts of the country and eleven other dogs, like Bear, ready and waiting at Guiding Eyes for blind masters and mistresses.

This book is the story of what happened in those first twenty-six days and in the weeks that followed. It is, on the surface, a simple story of hard work and discipline. From a sighted person's point of view, the daily victories—and failures—were small. After all, what's so difficult about picking up the harness handle of a guide dog and following him or her down the street? Not much if you're sighted. But what is it like for the blind?

Only a year ago, Tom Kalec was literally "living" in his bed, depressed and defeated by the loss of his sight, afraid to go out. And Bear, then only a puppy of six months, was winning blue ribbons in the show ring. Today, through Bear, Tom has regained part of what he lost when he lost his sight, and Bear has become not only Tom's eyes, but also his co-worker, his companion, and his friend. Tom and Bear are well on their way to independence, and Tom has a new eagerness about the future. And to greater and lesser degrees, it is the same for the other eleven students and dogs in the June class, and for many others like them who have already taken the steps or are waiting their turns.

The daily steps taken by each *are* small, but the final accomplishments are extraordinary victories, extraordinary expressions of the power of the human spirit and the animal spirit working together. Seeing, really seeing, is not just a function of the eyes and the brain. As the fox says in St. Exupery's fable *The Little Prince*, "It is only with the heart that one can see rightly; what is essential is invisible to the eye."

Tom & Bear

First Impressions

I arrived at Guiding Eyes for the Blind on the afternoon of Friday, June 6. The hour and a half drive up from New York, made with a friend, was mostly silent. I wanted to relax and let my mind quiet down, ease out of the city, and slowly settle into a different world.

My first impression of Guiding Eyes was of the serenity of the grounds, the warmth of the old house, now offices, and, above all, of the strength of the surrounding giant Norway spruce. It is a place of dignity and purpose.

Marty Yablonski, Coordinator of Student Admissions, greeted me warmly and showed me to my room in the student wing. The students are all due to arrive tomorrow, except for Bob, who is arriving on Monday after his high school graduation. The June class is an ideal training period for the younger students because it gives them two months of summer vacation after the training to gain experience with the dogs before going back to school.

Marty gave me copies of the profile sheets on each of the students so I could look them over this evening and get some idea of their individual backgrounds.

Don Weeks, the Apprentice Instructor responsible for the class, stopped by to introduce himself and say hello, and we ended up talking for a while. I explained to Don that I had a pretty good understanding of how dogs are trained to obey commands, but that what I couldn't understand about guide dog training is how the dogs are trained to take responsibility. "By building up their confidence, by giving them lots of praise," he said. "Confidence is the key, discipline and praise are the tools."

That evening I read over the profile sheets several times.

SHARON: Nineteen-year-old college student at SUNY. From the Bronx, New York. Cause of blindness: accident. Degree: total. Onset: 1965.

EILEEN: Twenty-two-year-old physical therapist from Manchester, New York. Cause of blindness: glaucoma. Degree: some light and color perception. Onset: birth.

JOYCE: Thirty-three-year-old mother from Abington, Massachusetts. Cause of blindness: diabetic retinopathy. Degree: occasionally some light perception. Onset: August, 1977.

ANITA: Twenty-seven-year-old mother of two young daughters. Completed one year of college. Diabetic. Cause of blindness: optic atrophy, cause unknown. Degree: less than 20/400, both eyes. Onset: 1965. Requests short-haired dog as one of her daughters has an allergy.

CAROLINE: Thirty-five-year-old doctoral student from Albany, New York. Cause of blindness: retinitis pigmentosa. Degree: shadow vision only. Onset: birth. Retrain.

BOB: Nineteen-year-old college student starting Boston College this fall. From Reading, Massachusetts. Cause of blindness: retinoblastoma. Degree: total. Onset: birth. Does not like German shepherds.

TOM: Twenty-four-year-old student from Columbia, South Carolina. Just completed five-month Personal Adjustment Program at the South Carolina Commission for the Blind. Cause of blindness: diabetic retinopathy. Degree: total. Onset: 1978.

JOE: Twenty-eight-year-old student who is married and lives with his wife in Richmond, Virginia. Cause of blindness: detached retinas. Degree: total. Onset: birth.

BILLY: Thirty-five-year-old employee of the Georgia Factory for the Blind in Atlanta, Georgia. Lives with his wife, Pat (also a graduate of Guiding Eyes), and young daughter. Cause of blindness: corneal dysplasia. Degree: total. Some vision until 1979. Onset: birth. Retrain. This will be Billy's second dog from GEB.

ROSS: Thirty-eight-year-old student working on his master's degree, from Huntington, West Virginia. Cause of blindness: diabetic retinopathy. Degree: total. Onset: 1967. Retrain. This will be Ross's third dog from GEB. Prefers a German shepherd.

HOWARD: Thirty-nine-year-old Vietnam veteran who lives with his wife and son in Colorado Springs, Colorado. Cause of blindness: atrophy of optic nerve, due to shrapnel wound. Degree: total (may fluctuate). Retrain. This will be Howard's third dog from GEB.

DAN: Fifty-five-year-old former welder for Con Edison who lives with his wife and three children in Rosedale, New York. Cause of blindness: optic atrophy. Degree: some light perception. Onset: December 1977. Dan is concerned about how the family dog will react to the new dog.

I tried to imagine what it's like to be blind. I closed my eyes for a few minutes and tried to walk around the room pretending. I tripped over a chair and instinctively opened my eyes. As long as I know I can open my eyes whenever I want to, can I really understand what it's like to be blind? I have a lot to learn, and tomorrow it all begins.

Twenty-Six Days of Training

SATURDAY, JUNE 7,
YORKTOWN HEIGHTS, NEW YORK

"Juno"

MORNING. The students began arriving around 10:00 A.M., driven to Guiding Eyes by families or friends, and coming by limousine in small groups from the New York airports. It was interesting to match the faces and personalities of the students with the profiles I had read last evening.

Apprentice Instructors Don Weeks and Brenda Schofield and Trainee Bill Seery helped the students with their baggage and showed them to their rooms, which have been carefully laid out to make life easier for the blind. Each room has a door that opens into the central hallway of the dorm and also a door that opens out onto the driveway. (This is for convenience in taking the dogs out to relieve themselves, "parking" as they call it here.) Since Guiding Eyes often serves multi-handicapped students with medical problems that need monitoring, each room also has an "assistance" call button near each bed, similar to those in hospitals. There is a small dispensary/lab at the end of the hall, and there is always a staff member on duty. The students were invited to relax and unpack until called for their "Juno Walks."

AFTERNOON. "Juno," by common agreement among guide dog trainers and professionals, is a fictitious, nonexis-

6

Instructor Don Weeks takes Tom on a "Juno Walk." Don plays the role of the guide dog to determine Tom's strength and pace.

tent guide dog that represents all guide dogs. Few, if any, real guide dogs will ever be named Juno.

During the Juno Walk, the instructor explains how to hold the harness handle and a few simple commands, like "Juno, forward," and then proceeds to take the role of the guide dog while walking the student around the grounds. At the end of the Juno Walk, the instructor explains how to use

Tom makes a left-handed leash correction.
It could have been stronger.

the leash to give corrections, by pulling sharply back on the leash while commanding the dog, "No!"

All of the students seemed to manage the Juno Walk quite well; all have reasonably good mobility, although some, especially the ones who haven't had a guide dog before, like Joyce and Joe, are a bit rigid. Perhaps that's just from being used to a cane, with which the body position *is* more erect and rigid. Eileen and Sharon both set quite a fast pace; they're ready to go! Some of the corrections are a little soft, Tom's for example, but Billy has it down; he's had a guide dog before.

EVENING. After dinner, the students assembled in the Campbell Lounge for the evening lecture.

For three months, Don and Brenda have been training the dogs, and tomorrow afternoon, a few short hours away, the students will receive their dogs; that's what they're waiting for! The early work is with obedience and teaching the commands used in guide dog work. Later in the training, the dogs are worked and reworked through every type of situation a blind person might conceivably face: streets, traffic, buses, subways, and so on. Now it is Don and Brenda's job, within twenty-six days, to make trainers out of each of the students. There is no magic to it, just hard work . . . and frustration. The dogs are just as capable of making mistakes as people are, and the place to make the mistakes is at Guiding Eyes, not back home.

During the three months of training, the dogs have become very attached to Don and Brenda and have accepted them as their masters. The main job for the first few days of work will be to get the dogs to "turn over" their affections and responses to the students. It will take time, but within four to five days, if all goes well, the dogs should begin to show the first signs of turning over their loyalties.

The dogs work for praise, so "praise your dog" is one of the first rules of guide dog work. And praise is not just mouthing words, it's enthusiasm and tone of voice. Consistency in what is expected of the dog is also essential. The dogs are trained to respond to certain commands, consistently. The students must be equally consistent in using them. Corrections, when properly used, show the dogs what is not acceptable and let them know what is expected. Through proper corrections, they learn respect. "The more you give your dog, the more your dog will give you. The more you meet his needs, the more he'll meet your needs."

Don and Brenda gave each of the students a new leash and showed them how to hold it properly, doubled over with the thumb on top, when "heeling" the dogs. And how to open it into a long leash for obedience training and play. Beginning tomorrow and for the first few days, the dogs are to be "heeled" at all times. The dogs have no responsibility when "heeling" other than to do it properly. The only

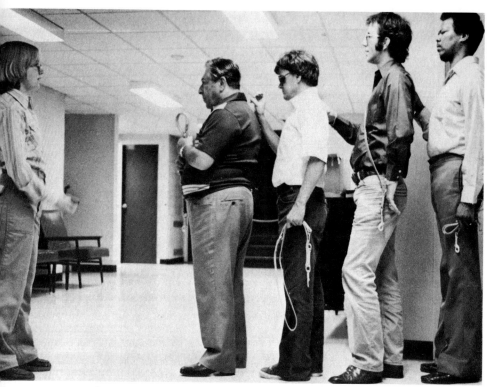

Instructor Brenda Schofield leads Dan, Howard, Ross, and Joe on a snakelike orientation walk through the building.

time a dog is "working" is when the student puts the dog in the harness and picks up the handle. That's when the dog carries his or her share of the responsibility.

Don and Brenda then explained the layout of the building and the relationship of the rooms, and divided the group in half. Each took half of the group on a snakelike orientation walk through the building, through the recreation room, the dining room, the offices, the lounges, and finally back to the students' rooms to finish any unpacking and get some sleep. Some had been up since 4:00 A.M. that morning.

MIDNIGHT. Don and Brenda let me sit in on the "matching" or pairing of the students with the dogs. Since Don and Brenda had trained the dogs for three months, they knew each of them inside out. They had trained a string of nineteen dogs for this class of twelve to give themselves some backup and some flexibility in matching.

From the Juno Walks this afternoon, Don and Brenda knew an amazing amount about each student. They knew the height, the weight, the pace, the arm strength, the balance and mobility, the voice and tone of commands and corrections, the personalities. And they knew, from asking the students, the basic routes and areas where they would use the dogs—country, city, or campus. (A dog that worries a bit on subways might be of limited use in the city but very acceptable in the country.)

The dogs are basically of two temperaments, "hard" and "soft." "Hard" dogs are dogs that can be a bit stubborn about taking commands, but on the other hand don't seem to be affected too seriously by quite a lot of correction. A "soft" dog can be a bit of a worrier and can become anxious and lose willingness over too many corrections. A "soft" dog can often be controlled with voice corrections and an occasional mild leash correction. A "hard" dog often requires strong leash corrections and an occasional bop on the nose.

Matching the right students with the right dogs seems a lot like casting a play, matching the right actors with the right parts. The students will spend every waking minute with their dogs for upwards of ten to twelve years. A good match of personalities and work patterns is crucial.

Finally, about 2:30 A.M., Don and Brenda had their list of suggested matches, with backup suggestions, ready to show Charlie Mondello, Class Supervisor, for his final approval. They decided to get some sleep and go over it again in the morning.

11

"Juno, come."

MORNING. Campbell Lounge. Geoff Lock, General Manager of Guiding Eyes, welcomed the students with an overview of guide dog work and training.

"First of all, a guide dog is not a miracle creature, just a regular dog that, in many instances, has been bred for this work, but with a regular dog's mind. It doesn't have a scaled-down human being's mind; it doesn't work like a little machine. You don't press a little button and it goes and press another little button and it stops. It really is an animal with all the little failings and frailties that any other dog would have.

"Therefore, if somebody comes to a guide dog school with not too good orientation and thinks that this dog is going to straighten him out in twenty-six days . . . In all honesty, if you can't find your way out of a paper bag when you come here, you aren't going to find your way out of a paper bag when you leave.

"The reason that a dog guides is that it has been trained to work a certain set of sequences. It understands that if it does this, it gets praise, and if it does that, it gets a correction. Some of it is instinctive, some of it is by constant repetition. It does it time after time after time, and it finally understands what it is required to do. But it is *trained* to do everything it does in guide dog work. And there's this funny little thing that anything that is trained can very quickly become untrained.

"Basically, most of the dogs we use come from our own breeding program; some come from outside sources. The types of dogs most commonly used, in this school anyway, are Labrador retrievers, both black and yellow; golden retrievers; some German shepherds (not a tremendous number, really; they can be very possessive); a few Bouvier des Flandres; an occasional collie; an occasional boxer; and an occasional crossbreed of any of these particular breeds."

Geoff closed by encouraging the students to work with the instructors and not to be concerned if, at first, the dogs "look round" for reinforcement from the instructors when students give commands. "Everyone in guide dog work has moments of frustration and difficulty. If you come with a genuine desire to get through the course, you'll be successful no matter what difficulties you may have."

Sue Harden, Director of Student Affairs (Sue is blind herself and works with a lovely yellow Lab named Jenny), gave a brief history of guide dogs. As early as 100 B.C., a blind Germanic king is said to have used a dog as a guide. A Rembrandt etching from the mid seventeenth century shows a little dog trying to pull the leg of his blind master, Tobias, toward an open doorway that Tobias has obviously misjudged. During and after World War I, the Germans began systematically training German shepherds as guides for blind war veterans, and after the war they continued to train them for civilians. In 1927, an American woman, Dorothy Eustis, who had been living in Switzerland and breeding German shepherds for several years, wrote an article for the *Saturday Evening Post*, which she called "The Seeing Eye." Two years later, she became one of the founders of the first American organization to train dogs as guides for the blind, which she also called The Seeing Eye. The school moved to Morristown, New Jersey, in 1932, and for the first time in 1942 enlisted the aid of 4-H families in raising puppies from the school's breeding program. Guiding Eyes for the Blind in Yorktown Heights, New York, was founded in 1956 by Donald Kauth, who is still the Executive Director.

Sue answered student questions and explained that Guiding Eyes is funded by private donations and that all the students' expenses for the training, including room and board and travel expenses, were paid for by Guiding Eyes. Students are, however, given an opportunity to donate $150 toward the cost of the dog if they can afford it. That's the first and last request the students will hear for money. Students were then asked to sign pledges that they would take care of their dogs and at no time, under any circumstances, use the dogs for begging.

Meanwhile, Don and Brenda met with Charlie in his office for about a half hour to go over the list of matches. Charlie suggested a few changes, which Don and Brenda readily agreed with, and then approved the new list. After the meeting Charlie told me that it often took a week or more to see how the matches were working out. Occasionally, changes are made.

NOON. Back in the Campbell Lounge, student excitement was running high. The moment they'd all been waiting for was just about to take place. After lunch, the students will receive their dogs, one at a time, in the lobby. They are to sit in a chair, give the command "Juno, come" (but using *their* dog's name), and Don or Brenda will then bring the dog over to them and help them attach the leash. They are then to take the dog back to their room and get acquainted by playing with it. They are not to let the dog off the leash.

Don and Brenda read off the list of teams, telling each student his or her dog's name and breed:

Sharon: Nolan, a black Lab
Eileen: Indy, a German shepherd
Joyce: Owen, a yellow Lab
Anita: Sue, a chocolate Lab
Caroline: Buffy, a golden retriever
Tom: Bear, a golden retriever
Joe: Tobias, a golden retriever

The dogs wait in the van before meeting their new masters. Bear is on the right with his nose out the window.

Billy: Denver, a black Lab
Ross: Lance, a yellow Lab
Howard: Marty, a golden retriever
Dan: Tucker, a golden retriever

Bob, who hasn't arrived yet, will be assigned a dog on Monday.

While the students ate Sunday dinner, Don, Brenda, and Bill went to the kennels to bathe and groom each of the dogs. The dogs were as excited as the students. The dogs were then loaded into one of the school vans and driven the few hundred yards to the dorm.

AFTERNOON. One by one, the students were called to the lobby from their rooms over the house PA system. As each

student sat down and called his or her dog, the instructor brought the dog over. There was then a flurry of fur, much laughter, and much petting and praise. Bear gave Tom a big kiss. Tom said he pictured Bear "with a big smile on his face." He took Bear back to his room and played with him by drying him off with a towel—Bear was still a bit damp from his bath. Bear loved it but kept trying to chew the towel.

4:00 P.M. Feed, water, and park. A lot of the dogs didn't eat very much—too much excitement—so getting them to "Get busy" during park time was a bit frustrating. Walking them back and forth by the curb helps stimulate the bowels and encourages them to get busy.

EVENING. Campbell Lounge. It took quite a while to get the dogs all quietly settled under the chairs, but this is a

Left: it is hard to say who is happier at their first meeting, Tom or Bear. Below: Bear hasn't quite figured out what's expected of him at "park" time. He will.

necessary part of the training. Back home, it is essential for the dog to lie quietly while a student is attending class or at work in an office or plant. Before the lecture Don warned Tom that "Bear is a chewer."

"Yes," Tom said, "I already know."

LECTURE. Tomorrow morning the students begin formal training with the dogs in Peekskill, a small town of less

Tom records the evening lecture on a special tape recorder made for the convenience of blind students. Bear rests quietly under his seat.

than 20,000 about twelve miles from the school. Don and Brenda had a lot of basic information to cover in tonight's lecture. But first the students were given harnesses for their dogs.

The harness consists of two parts: the harnesslike arrangement, which is worn by the dog, and the long rigid handle, which transmits the dog's messages to the student. When working, the dog wears both the harness and the leash, and both are held in the student's left hand.

While holding the harness handle, the student should keep his or her left arm straight, but not rigid. The elbow should be slightly bent and the wrist relaxed. A rule of thumb, literally, is to keep the left thumb down by the seam edge of the left pants pocket. This is a low point of contact, the left hand roughly halfway between the thigh and knee, so it is natural at first to have some difficulty maintaining balance.

The harness handle not only sends messages from the dog to the student, but it also acts as a shock absorber of sorts. Dogs are horizontal animals and people are vertical animals whose whole bodies move up and down with each step. Dogs, being four-legged, have four points of contact with the ground and tend to walk more smoothly. Therefore, the harness handle is attached to the harness with rings that permit it to move and absorb some of the shock created between the dog's gait and the student's walk. This is also why the student's left wrist and elbow must be relaxed, not rigid.

Learning to walk smoothly with a dog is a lot like learning a new language or learning to dance with a new partner: it takes time to learn and understand all the little subtleties.

Amazingly, there are only a few basic commands in guide dog work: "forward," "right," "left," "straight," and "hup-up." Always use the dog's name, to make sure he's paying attention, before giving a command. "Juno, forward!" There

19

are only two times when the dog's name is not used before a command: when the dog is given a "No!" or a correction, and when the dog is commanded to "Stay!" The dog's name is never associated with negatives like "No!" In the case of "Stay!", by calling the dog's name first, the dog is alerted that he is to do something and then is told to "Stay"—sort of a contradiction of commands.

Guide dogs are trained to go from one curb to the next and to stop at each curb. It is the student's job to find each curb with his or her left foot and then "tap it out," by tapping the curb with the left foot several times. "Tapping" calls the dog's attention to the curb and lets the dog know the student has found it. The student should always remember to give the dog lots of praise for doing his job.

TOMORROW. The students will work the dogs in harness, with Don, Brenda, Charlie, and Bill beside and behind them. They will each walk one square block in Peekskill, all right turns, no street crossings. One square block.

The rule: "Follow your dog. Learn to move with the motion of the dog."

MONDAY, JUNE 9, PEEKSKILL, NEW YORK

"Juno, forward!"

MORNING. Students were divided into two groups. Five went with Don in one van and six went with Brenda in a second van. The dogs sat facing the students who used their knees and legs to brace the dogs. It's about a fifteen-minute drive into Peekskill, and there was much anticipation about the day ahead.

The vans pulled up in front of an old house at 1122 Main Street, where Guiding Eyes owns the basement as a small

The Guiding Eyes lounge and rest area on Main Street in Peekskill, New York.

lounge and rest area for the students and instructors. Soon part of the first floor will be available. Students and dogs spend quite a bit of time there, waiting their turns with instructors.

The route for the morning was one square block, starting with a right turn from the lounge on Main Street and continuing with right turns at each corner until back at the starting point.

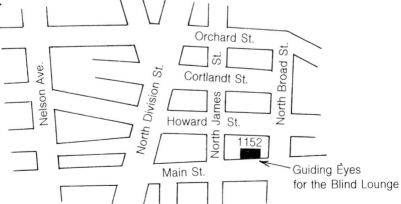

21

Brenda guides Tom and Bear through their first in-harness steps together. Trainee Bill Seery follows behind.

To make a right turn, give the command "Juno, right," accompanied by a hand gesture to the right, move your left foot away from the curb, and turn your body 90° to the right. Wait for the dog to move forward, as there may be an obstruction, such as a telephone pole or traffic sign, to go around. All hand gestures are done with the right arm kept low in front of the body so as to be within the dog's vision.

Everyone made it around the block in good shape. Most made several practice turns at each corner. It could have

In making their first right turn, Brenda makes certain that Tom taps out the curb and follows Bear around the traffic sign.

been a lot steadier, especially for the students who haven't had a guide dog before, but everyone made it, and with a lot of the joy and pleasure of a kid mastering a solo ride on his first two-wheeler.

Tom told me that he "loved every minute of it," and that it was "the first time he'd really walked at a normal pace" since before he went blind. With Bear he can walk normally again, or almost normally. "It's so much different than it is with a cane. With a cane you have to keep your body rigid and walk slowly, feeling your way along. I didn't like the cane."

At the end of their first walk together, Brenda encourages Tom to give Bear lots of praise.

NOON. The vans brought us back to Guiding Eyes for lunch and an hour of rest. The last student, Bob, arrived this morning while we were in Peekskill and after a Juno walk, he was assigned Raft, a black Lab.

AFTERNOON. Repeat of the morning one-square-block exercise. Students are a little more relaxed, beginning to get the hang of it. The dogs are still watching and listening to Don and Brenda most of the time, as was expected.

EVENING. Don and Brenda answered questions. A few dogs did quite a bit of chewing last night. "Dogs chew when they get lonely." They were used to the kennel and their kennelmates. Keep them on their bedchains and put things out of their reach. As for letting passers-by come up and pet the dogs, as happened several times in Peekskill today, it's not advisable but it is also often hard to stop. Try explaining that the dog is working when he is in harness and shouldn't be distracted. Try to be pleasant about it; guide dog users want to have a good image with the public.

LECTURE. Most guide dogs walk down the middle of the sidewalks, giving good clearance on both sides. Some dogs may tend to hug the building line a little more than others. No animal, including man, walks in perfectly straight lines, so pick up the left and right motion of the dog and move with him. Follow your dog! Walk a little slower than your dog; keep tension on the handle so he can guide you.

If your right side brushes against a bush, slap your right leg with your right hand to call the dog's attention to the problem and say, "No, left!" Then give the dog lots of praise; he's a good dog when he gives you good clearance. For praise, the tone is cheerful and encouraging. Praise the dog when you approach a curb; make him *want* to get to the curb. "Your dog wants to do things for you because he gets praised! Praise accomplishes two things: It encourages the dog, and it raises his level of willingness to work."

TOMORROW. The same square block but this time it will be all *left* turns. For a left turn, locate and "tap out" the curb with the left foot, same as for right turns. Then pull the left foot and handle back at the same time, moving the dog back out of the way, turn 90° left so that you are perpendicular to the dog, giving the voice command, "Juno, left," along with a hand gesture to the left, and take the first step forward with the right foot.

TUESDAY, JUNE 10, PEEKSKILL

"Juno, left."

MORNING. For most of the students, left turns are harder and clumsier. Three things to do at once: pull back on the harness handle and the left foot, give the voice and hand signal, and pivot the body 90°. The students who have had dogs before handled the turns pretty well but need some adjustment to the new dogs. The others are going to have to work at it to get it down.

At the end of the square-block route the students finish up back at the lounge. They must learn to locate the opening for the steps, which are on the left. The technique here is "suggesting" a left to the dog. As a student comes to within a few paces of the lounge, he or she must give the command "Left, left. Left, left," accompanied by a hand gesture to the left. It is up to the student to develop a sense through use of landmarks when he or she is "a few paces" from the lounge. When the dog finds the steps (and it will take some repetition), he stops; the student must then tap out the step with his left foot, and give the dog lots of praise. That is how the dog is trained to find entrances in the middle of the block; by suggesting a "Left, left," or a "Right, right." After he's worked an opening or a door or a driveway several times, the dog may begin to anticipate it. The dog should not get in the habit of anticipating what the student is going to do; it eventually leads to problems. The student may not always want to stop at that particular opening or door.

Joyce had a mild diabetic reaction toward the end of her walk with Owen. Her blood sugar began to drop and she began to feel a bit wobbly. Don sat her down on the steps in front of the lounge and brought her some orange juice,

Left turns require several actions at once; neither Tom nor Bear is very certain at first.

26

a quick way to bring the sugar level back up. Within ten minutes she was feeling much better.

There are four diabetics in the class: Tom, Joyce, Anita, and Ross. Guiding Eyes is equipped to handle their special needs—draw insulin shots, test urine samples for sugar, and handle emergencies. The diabetics get special diets according to their individual needs, and fruit juice or sugar cubes are available to them at all times, in the lounges or in the vans. During class exercises Charlie, Don, Brenda, and Bill all carry tubes of instant glucose for emergencies.

NOON. Yesterday working with the dogs all seemed like a piece of cake to most of the students. Just getting around the block was an exhilarating experience. This morning I think they realized that it is going to take some hard work. Billy, a student who has had a few years' experience with guide dogs, brought home the point at lunch: "The dog is only your eyes. It's as if you were driving a car. *You* have to pay attention to the road, *you* have to be alert, *you* have to know where you're going, and *you* have to make all the decisions."

AFTERNOON. Same square block, same left turns. A little better. Students concentrating more.

Charlie, the class supervisor, told me he saw signs already that several of the dogs were beginning to turn over to the students. The dogs are starting to pay more attention to the students, they are starting out at a faster, more confident pace. They're watching Don and Brenda less and wagging their tails more.

EVENING. At the start of the evening lecture, the students were given grooming combs and brushes for their dogs. Some of the dogs are scratching. They should be told "No!" immediately and stopped. Dogs are capable of irritating the

Tom uses the correct arm signal for a left turn, but Bear is still looking to Brenda for commands.

skin badly; their nails are capable of breaking the skin, which can lead to an infection. Some veterinarians say that 80 percent of all dogs' skin problems are due to scratching. Grooming stimulates the skin like a good massage, removes dead hairs, and reduces odor. Most dogs love it and it should become a daily habit, just like washing your face. It is especially important for blind people to groom their dogs daily

29

Don holds Bear's head while Tom brushes out Bear's coat. Tom is gentle; Bear is patient.

because it gives them a chance to feel for bumps or sores or cuts that they might not otherwise notice. And most importantly, a well-groomed dog shows the public that the dog is special, that you handle and care for your dog, that you can be independent and take care of yourself and your dog's needs.

The students were also given a supply of heartworm pills, given routinely to all dogs during the mosquito season, and shown how to give the daily pill. It is given just before feeding in the morning. The food is then a reward, of sorts, for any discomfort. Command the dog to a sitting position. With one hand on top of the dog's head, pinch the skin around and under his upper teeth; that way he has to bite through his own skin before he can bite you. With the other hand, stick the pill as far back on the dog's tongue as you can reach. Close his mouth and hold it closed. Hold his head up in the air while stroking his throat to make him swallow. When he does, give him praise, and his food.

Don and Brenda observed that some of the dogs were pulling and straining, getting too far out in front of the students. It is much easier to follow the dog's motions if he's beside you. Some of the right-handed students may need to build up a little more strength in their left arms.

Some of the dogs are goofing off once in a while or not taking the students all the way to the curb, stopping anywhere from five to ten feet from it. The command to use in both situations is "Hup-up!" With "Hup-up" you use the same hand signal as with "forward," a forward motion of the right hand and arm. "Hup-up" tells the dog one of three things: (1) "Take me all the way up to the curb or obstacle so that I can tap it with my foot," or (2) "Stop fooling around or goofing off; get working!" or (3) "Get going faster," as it is also used when a dog's pace becomes too slow or lethargic.

TOMORROW. Tomorrow's route in Peekskill will contain the first street crossings, four of them. This is where the student's previous training in Orientation and Mobility (O & M) at his or her local Commission for the Blind really becomes important. Dogs are color blind and, contrary to most of the public's conception of guide dogs, do not understand or pay attention to traffic signals or lights. The student makes the decision when to cross, from listening to the flow of traffic.

Class adjourned to the Grooming Room adjacent to the Campbell Lounge. Don and Brenda work with the students individually, showing them how to groom the dogs by starting at the head and working back.

31

First crossings

MORNING. An expanded version of the one square block. All right turns, four crossings.

Coming up to a traffic light–controlled intersection, the student taps out the curb with his left foot and praises the dog. He listens to the traffic as he was trained to do in Orientation and Mobility, using the sound of parallel traffic to make sure his body is facing straight ahead. When he hears the perpendicular traffic, the traffic crossing in front of him, stop *and* parallel traffic start up, he knows that he has the green light. If he's uncertain, he waits another full cycle of traffic and lights. When he's ready to cross, he gives the command "Juno, forward." He steps down into the street in a smooth and confident manner with his right foot, and moves across the street at a good pace. This is not the time to be slow! While crossing the street, he uses the command, "Straight," with the same hand gesture as forward, arm raised, and mixes it with praise. "Straight, straight. Attaboy, Juno, straight."

When across the street, the dog stops at the upcurb. (The step up from the street to the sidewalk is called an "upcurb"; the step down from the sidewalk to the street, a "down-curb.") The student taps out the curb with his left foot and praises the dog. "Good boy, Juno." He gives the command "Juno, forward," and steps up with his right foot. The handle is never, under any circumstances, dropped in the middle of the street; it tells the dog he is "off duty."

With excellent peripheral vision, the dog has good aware-ness of traffic that may be turning into the street from the side. The dog will not obey the command "Juno, forward," if he is wary or thinks it isn't safe. In guide dog work, this is referred to as "intelligent disobedience." And he will

Brenda guides Tom and Bear through their first street crossing, making certain Tom urges Bear to keep moving straight.

pull back out of the way quickly if a car turns too close.

As a sighted person, I expected that crossing a street would be the most potentially fearful of all situations for the blind. I hadn't realized, at first, that all the students had taken previous training in Orientation and Mobility and, from working with canes, already knew how to use traffic sounds to cross streets and intersections. They all handled this morning's crossings calmly, although some students lurched forward rather abruptly in their efforts to cross quickly and Joyce dropped Owen's handle when she heard a car coming. Fortunately, they were in no danger. Some students had difficulty keeping their bodies facing straight ahead and tended to let their crossings drift off to one side.

Confidence is clearly the key to guide dog work. The more confident the student is or becomes, the more confidently the dog works. And the more confidently the dog works, the more confidently the student works. The students are giving the dogs a lot of praise to build their confidence, and the dogs are beginning to give the students their loyalty and love.

NOON. Last night Sharon discovered a sizable bump or growth on Nolan's left hind leg while she was grooming him and Charlie thinks the vet should look at it. The vet applied some medication and a bandage and wants to see Nolan again on Friday.

AFTERNOON. Same expanded walk but using all left turns. Tom notices that Bear is crossing in front of him at curbs and intersections, making it hard for Tom to step off the curb in a straight line. "I had it all wrong about Bear. I thought he'd be perfect, like Superman. I just assumed he'd always go straight." Charlie told him to give Bear a bop on the nose if he keeps crossing in front of him. Tom finally did, but I think corrections could be a problem for Tom. Bear is a bit of a "worrier," and he's so gentle that Tom doesn't feel much like giving him corrections or a bop on the nose. "The only thing I worried about coming to Guiding Eyes was that I was going to love my dog too much," Tom said to me at one point. He also feels that he needs to build up his left arm. He's not keeping Bear back beside him as far as he should.

Don stresses to Joyce the importance of body alignment at the down-curb.

Don, Brenda, and Bill are dropping back a pace or two and giving fewer reinforcing commands. The dogs are definitely turning over now.

EVENING. Lecture. In the first days of training, while the students and dogs are getting to know one another, too many corrections from the students might upset the dogs and slow down the turn-over process. But now that the dogs are turning over, it is time to start bearing down on corrections when necessary. There are two types of corrections, verbal and leash. "No" is the first command the dog ever learns. He knows what it means . . . when you say it like you mean it.

35

There are three types of leash corrections. A right-handed correction is for distractions to the dog's left or up ahead. With the right hand, pull the leash sharply out to your right, which pulls the dog away from the distraction on the left. Left-handed leash corrections are for distractions on the right or up ahead and are done by stopping and dropping the harness handle and then pulling back sharply on the leash with the left hand. A two-handed jerk on the leash is used when nothing else works.

If the choke chain is resting properly low on the dog's neck, and not around his throat, a leash correction does not hurt the dog. The muscles in the lower neck are quite powerful, like the human thigh. In fact, too many leash corrections will build up stronger muscles in the dog's neck, and the corrections will be less effective. Corrections should come as a surprise to the dog. One good correction is worth a thousand nags!

Appropriate corrections are a good way of gaining a dog's respect. Most dogs will try to test you once in a while or goof off or fail to give you enough clearance. For the most part, they know they're doing it and they will respect you for the correction. When a dog has responded to the correction and done what you've wanted him to, always praise him. On the other hand, don't overdo it. Too much praise gets the dog all excited and he thinks it's playtime. The dog should get lots of praise but he should also have to work for it.

TOMORROW. One-mile walk, six crossings. There will be more distractions on the walk, more pets and stray dogs, bumpier sidewalks, and more garbage cans to go around.

THURSDAY, JUNE 12, PEEKSKILL

"Juno, straight."

MORNING AND AFTERNOON. Expanded walk, one mile, six crossings. Morning, right turns only; afternoon, left turns only.

The right turns are smoothing out pretty well for most of the students, but some of the left turns still need work. Some students are turning their bodies too far and almost making U-turns. Most of the dogs paid very little attention to the strays and barking wonders along North Broad Street; they'd been over this route many times with the trainers

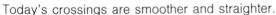

Today's crossings are smoother and straighter.

and pretty well knew what was coming and what was expected. A few needed leash corrections as reminders.

EVENING. Lecture. Guide dogs are trained to follow a simple pattern of sequences. They are also trained to use a limited amount of intelligent disobedience, for those instances when they see or sense something that would make their master's command unsafe. It is conceivable that if a dog is allowed to use too much disobedience or is allowed to anticipate commands consistently and get away with it, he could end up paying no attention at all to commands. To avoid the possibility and to help keep a proper balance of discipline, the students are shown a simple set of obedience exercises, the dog's "daily dozen."

Obedience training is performed with the dog on the long leash and is a mixture of commands like "Juno, sit. Juno, down. Stay. Juno, come." Appropriate hand and leash signals accompany the voice command if necessary. Always praise the dog when he obeys your commands.

Dogs are descended from wolves. Before they were domesticated, dogs lived in packs like wolves, with a leader to which all members gave their loyalty. As the leader was always the strongest of all the dogs in the pack, he was also the most vulnerable. He was the one who fought off challengers and enemies, and led the hunt. Of all the dogs, he was the one most in danger of being injured or killed. Consequently, members of the pack had to learn to transfer their loyalty from the old leader to the new several times in their lifespan. The transfer was usually much easier for a younger dog than an older dog.

Today, the dog looks on its master as its leader, which is one of the reasons why dogs are so successful in guide work. They have a natural instinct for loyalty and obedience, and a natural ability to transfer that loyalty from one leader to another, such as from trainer to student.

Frequently now, Bear crosses his head in front of Tom to protect him from stepping off the down-curb, but it also makes Tom turn his body and lose his body alignment at the crossing.

Using the long leash, Tom gives Bear the obedience command to "stay!"

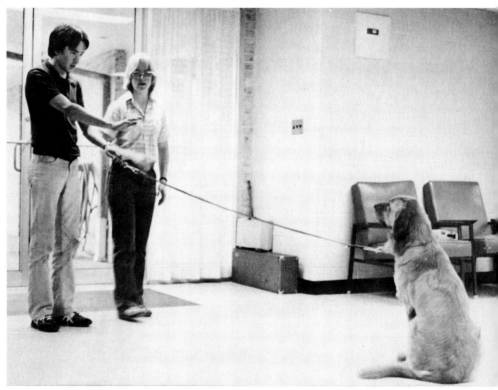

Some dogs are by size and nature more challenging and stubborn than others: the "hard" dogs. And some dogs are more docile and obedient: the "soft" dogs. Neither extreme is desirable in guide dog work. But within the extremes there is quite an acceptable range and variation. Dogs are naturally just as individual as people.

Starting tonight after the lecture and for the next several nights, Don and Brenda will be going over obedience training and testing with each student, one at a time. It's an essential discipline.

The dogs continue to show good signs of turning over, and the matches are all looking good at this stage of the training.

TOMORROW. The mile walk, but in matched pairs. Two students and two dogs matched for pace.

FRIDAY, JUNE 13, PEEKSKILL

Matched pairs

MORNING. The procedure for working with a partner: One partner takes the lead and waits at the downcurb for the other partner to catch up. That partner then crosses the street or turns first, taking over the lead for the next block. Each partner has the lead every other block. If the change-over involves a street crossing, one partner crosses, taps out the curb, moves forward about ten paces, and stops. He then calls back to his partner to let him know he's across, and waits until he hears from his partner that he is. Then he gives the dog the command "Forward" and takes the lead for the rest of that block.

Every dog wants to be in the lead; expect some competitive spirit. The lead dog is likely to keep looking back and the

Above: working as partners, Tom and Caroline cross Howard Street. Tom and Bear crossed first, took ten steps forward, and stopped to wait for Caroline and Buffy. For the block ahead, Caroline will pass Tom and take the lead. Below: this time Caroline crosses first. She carefully follows Buffy around the truck parked in the crosswalk.

second dog is likely to keep pulling to catch up. Watch for it and keep it under control. Be ready to give a leash correction if the dog looks back too much and a "Steady," by pushing down on the handle, if he's pulling too hard or too fast.

NOON. Nolan is back from the vet with his foot all bandaged again. The vet decided to operate and remove the growth, which went clear to the bone. So no more work for Nolan until at least Monday.

AFTERNOON. Same walk, left turns. Some partners were switched around. Tom and Bear worked with Caroline and Buffy this afternoon. There was a line for confession going into the Episcopal church and Bear decided to stop and get

Nolan is relatively
unconcerned
by his new bandage.

42

into the line. That was quite a surprise! Tom was really happy about the way Bear stopped at the bumps or large cracks in the sidewalks along Orchard Street; he is getting a real sense that Bear is "watching out" for him.

By working in pairs, the students are beginning to work things out for themselves and take responsibility for each other. That way it is possible for Don, Brenda, and Charlie to drop farther behind. Some of the crossings still aren't very straight, and left turns are still presenting problems.

EVENING. There was no lecture this evening, but there will be obedience checks again. Joyce left the dinner table very tired and frustrated and broke into tears. Everyone is tired. The crankiness that comes with tiredness makes everyone seem a little more human after the really superhuman efforts of the past week. Also there's a rumor going around, probably started by one of the retrains who knows the course, that tomorrow is a one-mile solo walk around Peekskill.

SATURDAY, JUNE 14, PEEKSKILL
Solo pairs

MORNING. The rumor was true. This morning the students took their first solo walks—without instructors at their sides, but in pairs. The route is the mile walk in Peekskill, which they have been working for the past two days.

There was a lot of nervous anticipation in the Peekskill lounge and Charlie, wisely, cracked a few jokes to break some of the tension. Permanent pairs were assigned.

The instructors took various positions along the route where one of them could always see what was happening; Bill started off the pairs at five-minute intervals. The diabetics, like Tom, are always taken first, as there is less danger

Left: Tom and Dan are now permanent partners. They talk over the route before starting out on their solo walk. Above: starting off down Main Street, Bear and Tucker are both temporarily distracted by a puppy.

of a low blood sugar reaction shortly after breakfast or lunch than there is in the late morning or late afternoon.

Tom and Dan, now permanent partners, were to go first. They discussed the points along the route, making sure of each crossing and turn. When they had it clear in their minds, they wished each other luck and Dan and Tucker led off. Dan would wait for Tom at the North James Street downcurb and let Tom cross over first, taking over the lead for the next block.

Tom and Dan took their time, stopped at each downcurb to discuss the next moves, and showed good concentration. They make a good team. There were no real problems and the walk looked remarkably good. Tucker works better when

Left: Tom and Bear head straight across Howard Street on the second leg of the solo walk. Right: Tom and Bear maneuver a smooth right turn at Orchard and North Broad streets.

he and Dan have the lead. When Tom and Bear have the lead, Tucker's competitive instinct comes to the fore and he starts pulling and straining to catch up. Dan corrected him with the leash several times. Instincts can be inhibited to some extent, but they are always there.

Tom and Dan were both very proud of their dogs and gave them lots of attention and praise when they reached the steps of the lounge. Tom can't get over how Bear watches out for him. Dan all of a sudden has realized that he and Tucker can work together on their own. Since losing most of his sight two years ago, he's stayed at home most of the time, not wanting to go out. Tucker has given him new hope that he can be more independent again.

Safely back at the lounge, Bear and Tucker get lots of praise.

NOON. At lunch the victories of the morning were all re-lived. All the students had worked the route safely and effec-tively; the fine points will come with time and more practice. To go from a Juno Walk last Saturday to a mile solo today seems like an amazing feat of hard work and courage on everyone's part, the instructors', the students', and the dogs'. The feeling of victory is well deserved.

There is to be a short lecture in the Campbell Lounge after lunch, and then the rest of the day is free.

LECTURE. Up until now the students have been "heeling" their dogs everywhere, only working them in harness during walks in class. Now they are to start working the dogs around the dorm and house areas of Guiding Eyes, into and out of the vans, and around the lounge area in Peekskill. This will give them much more independence.

Students are to stop at all steps, stairs, and doors, tap

them out with foot or hand to let the dogs know that they have located them, and then praise the dogs.

Guide dogs are valuable, as the students are beginning to learn. Guiding Eyes tattoos the inner right rear leg of all its guide dogs with the Guiding Eyes social security number, which is registered with the National Dog Registry as a permanent means of identification if the dog is lost or stolen. This afternoon Don and Brenda checked each of the dogs for a clearly readable tattoo.

EVENING. Many of the students slept most of the afternoon. I did too. We ordered pizza and soda or beer and turned the rec room into a cabaret. Dan introduced us to a game he'd made in his workshop at home; he calls it Hi Rollers. The game board is in braille, and soon the dice and pennies were flying. Billy, one of the students, was the big loser: 83 cents. Sharon and Bob took turns playing the piano and singing in the Campbell Lounge. Most of us were still tired and turned in early.

End of the first week of training.

SUNDAY, JUNE 15, YORKTOWN HEIGHTS

Tom

MORNING. Geoff Lock, General Manager of Guiding Eyes and the man responsible for all the day-to-day operations of the school, lives in a house next door. I often see him walking across the lawn to the school in the mornings. I thought it might be a good time to catch him for a few minutes; I wanted his permission to focus more on Tom and Bear.

Tom is a diabetic, and diabetes is the number one cause of new cases of blindness in the United States today. He lost his sight two years ago, so he's been blind a relatively

47

short time. I think that what Tom has been through, and is going through here, must be very much like what a lot of blind people go through. Tom is friendly and outgoing and doesn't seem to mind talking about himself or answering questions.

When I caught up with Geoff, he was full of encouragement, as he always is. He's a real confidence builder, in dogs and people.

LATE AFTERNOON. I took Tom and Bear for a walk around the grounds of Guiding Eyes. I haven't had much experience as a sighted guide and felt a little clumsy at first. Tom put me at ease by showing me how to let him put the fingers of his right hand just above my left elbow. In that way he can feel the rhythm and motion of my body and follow me much in the way he follows Bear. He uses my arm much like the harness handle.

Tom's last name is Kalec; it's a Czechoslovakian name. Tom's father is from Iowa, where his grandparents still live on a small farm. His mother is from Japan so Tom considers himself "half Japanese." As Tom likes to say, he was "made in California and born in Texas" in August, 1956. He's almost twenty-four. He has an older sister, Lila, twenty-six; a younger sister, Nina, twenty-two; and two younger brothers, Mike, nineteen, and Ronald, seven. Tom's dad was in the Army and so Tom was an "Army brat" most of his life. He's lived on Army bases in Germany and Japan and now lives in Columbia, South Carolina, near Fort Jackson.

Tom knew he wanted a guide dog as soon as he first started to accept his blindness; it became his goal. He knew that most guide dog schools require Orientation and Mobility training (basically, cane travel) first, although it's not absolutely mandatory at Guiding Eyes. But Tom felt he needed to know how to use a cane before he got a dog. Many of the skills would be useful and he'd know how to use the cane if the dog ever got sick and couldn't work for any length of time. Two weeks earlier Tom completed a five-month Personal Adjustment Program at the South Carolina Commission for the Blind, which included Orientation and Mobility.

Tom first heard about Guiding Eyes when a field representative, Steve Kotun, visited the Commission in February. Tom wanted a dog as soon as he finished his training at the Commission in May, and Steve helped him process his application. "The day that I received the call that I had been accepted—just two weeks before June seventh—was one of the happiest days of my life."

One of Tom's biggest fears before going to the Commission was that he thought it would take him forever to learn his way around. He was amazed; it only took him two or three days to learn how to get to all his classes. He learned how to hear walls and listen to openings.

"At first I didn't know I could do it. I'd be walking down the halls and my instructor would say, 'Pay attention. Listen real closely now and tell me when you hear a difference.' So I'd start concentrating and concentrating and I *would* hear a difference. I could hear openings, doors, intersecting passageways. You can too. Close your eyes in the hallways of the dorm and try it."

There's a pretty common misconception that when you lose one sense, like sight, your other senses get better. Tom doesn't think that is true. He doesn't think you actually hear better, he thinks you learn to listen better. You pay more attention to sounds and learn to distinguish subtle differences. Eventually you don't even have to concentrate; it comes automatically. Tom can walk into a room and *hear* the size of it, and can walk down the center of a hallway by balancing the sound of the walls on the left with the sound on the right.

I asked Tom if he ever counted his steps. Counting is another misconception. "If you count steps you'll have so many numbers in your mind you'll get them all confused. And if you get distracted and lose count then you don't know where you are. It's much better to listen, and use landmarks."

In O & M, Tom wasn't given a cane right away. First he was taught to use the "upper arm, forearm position," the right forearm held out and across the face to protect the head and body. "It feels funny, like you're going to give a karate chop. But it's better than banging your head," he said.

50

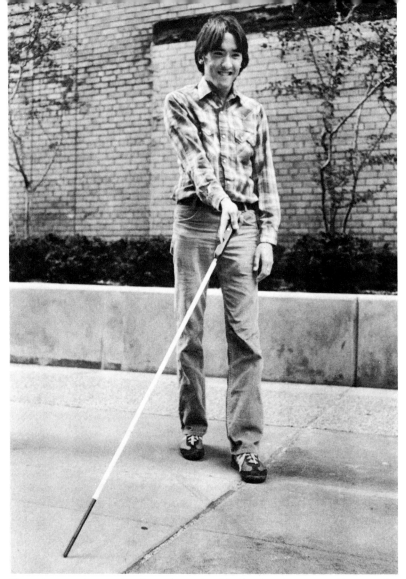

Tom demonstrates the "touch method" of using the cane. No wonder his wrist would get tired and sore.

Tom's first training with the cane was in the "diagonal technique" where the cane is held diagonally across the body for protection against running into things. "I practiced the diagonal technique for quite a while; I had to get used to the feel and weight of the cane. Then I learned the 'touch method,' the technique you use for walking around. My wrist would be so tired and sore from holding my arm stiff and just using the wrist motion to move the cane! And I had to get used to making the arc just the width of my body and keeping the cane in the center of my body. It takes a lot of time and practice. And I dreaded most of it. I felt so conspicuous. Even now with the cane I'm still self-conscious about it. But that's just me. Some blind people prefer a cane. You can hang a cane in the closet or fold it up and put it in your pocket, but you have to make space in your life for a dog. It's a big responsibility."

As part of his training with the cane Tom learned how to use traffic sounds and flow to cross streets and keep his body facing straight ahead, to use landmarks for orientation, and how to make accurate 90° turns—techniques all useful to him now in working with Bear. But coming from a cane to a dog, there are some adjustments to make too. For instance, with a cane you always start out on your left foot, but with the dog you always start out on your right foot. The cane is always held with the right hand, the harness handle with the left hand, leaving the right hand free. Tom stopped and asked me to hold out my arms. He felt my right forearm and then the left and said immediately, "You're right handed." I asked him how he knew that. "The muscle in your right arm is more developed. You use it more." Simple really, but I was caught by surprise. I'm used to seeing.

During his five months at the Commission, Tom had several other classes, such as braille. Braille is a system in which raised dots in any of six positions or combinations stand for letters and numbers. "At first it's hard trying to translate dots into letters. It's like learning a foreign language. But after a lot of practice, I don't think of letters any more. It's funny how the brain can adapt to things like that," he explained.

In Home Management class Tom learned simple and safe cooking techniques, how to put braille tags in pants and shirts so he could tell their colors, how to use signature cards and check forms.

Tom already knew how to type, so he didn't need the typing class. But he did take an art class. For a project he sculpted a self-portrait out of clay all by feeling the dimensions of his head. His teacher wanted him to paint it realistically but Tom wanted to leave it white "like the Greeks or Romans." Everyone told him it looked like George Washington. When he took the bust home the family was surprised. "Did *you* do that?" Tom wants to know why everyone is so surprised when blind people do things. "Blind people can do lots of things. Just because we use a cane or a sighted guide or a guide dog doesn't mean we're helpless."

Tom thinks that in some ways there are advantages in being blind. "People go by sight too much. They look at a person and say, 'Oh, look at him!' When you're blind you can't do that; you can't judge a book by its cover." Tom remembers that when he was sighted he was very shy, afraid to meet people and talk to them. Now that he's blind he talks to everyone.

And Tom learns about people now by listening to them, really listening. He tries to sense who they are and hear what they feel from the words they use and their tone of voice. As he and Bear get closer and closer, Tom feels that most of the time he can sense what Bear is thinking about. "Like now." Tom reached down for Bear, who was lying asleep at his feet. "I can feel him now. He's at peace; he knows I'm here. He follows me everywhere I go, waits in the bathroom while I take a shower. He's not at peace if I'm not around. It's the same with me, too, when I'm not around Bear. There's a bond of love between us, like he's part of me and I'm part of him. Bear and I are together now."

Tomorrow begins the second week of training.

Traffic checks

MORNING. Waiting for class to begin in the Peekskill lounge, everyone had the feeling that something was more or less up. The retrains suspected traffic checks but didn't say much. And traffic checks it was!

The students were instructed to work with their partners and take the long Cortlandt Street route using all left turns. As the students approached the intersection of Howard and North Broad, Charlie was waiting nearby in a running car. As a student started to cross, Charlie sped across his path and jammed on the brakes, squealing tires and all. Next, as the students continued on North Broad, Charlie parked the car across the sidewalk with the motor running. Charlie, of course, remained in the car. The point was that when a car is blocking your path, make sure to listen for the motor. If it's running, there is obviously potential danger.

A few of the students got quite a surprise, Joyce especially. They were reminded there really is traffic out there! But the dogs were remarkably cool, pulling the students back out of the way—with the exception of Billy's Denver. Denver got the shakes and never did really settle down.

The traffic checks didn't bother Tom and Bear at all. Tom obviously already has great confidence in Bear and the instructors. The first two times Tom was a little slow stepping back, although Bear was pulling him back. "Bear did the right thing. I just didn't follow him. Like they always tell us, 'Follow your dog.' "

AFTERNOON. At noon, Charlie decided that Denver had to be "retired"; they simply couldn't take a chance that he might panic again in traffic. In exchange for Denver, Billy was given Dolly, a calm and especially steady golden re-

Traffic check!

triever. As a retrain, Billy should have little trouble adjusting quickly to Dolly.

OBSTACLES. The students were told to use the same route they had used in the morning. Meanwhile Bill and Don were setting up a series of obstacles on North Broad Street and along Cortlandt.

The students were reminded that whenever the dog stops it is for a reason and it is up to the student to find out the reason. The technique is to keep your right foot firmly in place and to slide the left foot forward. If the left foot then strikes the obstacle or the edge of the curb, praise the dog. If the left foot does not find the obstacle, it is possible that

the dog has stopped for an overhanging obstacle that is too low to pass under safely. Reach out with your right hand and slowly bring it down in front of you, starting at head height. If you still don't discover the obstacle, give a couple of "Hup-ups," which, in this case, tell the dog to take you closer. When you find the curb or obstacle, tap it out and praise the dog.

Three obstacles were set up. The first was an overhanging bar about head height, with a piece of foam around it for protection. It would be easy for the dog to pass under, but if he didn't go around it automatically or stop, it would bop the student in the head. The second obstacle was a sawhorse that completely blocked the sidewalk and extended almost

Left to right:

Aware of the first obstacle, the overhang, Bear leads Tom carefully around it.

Bear stops at the second obstacle and Tom reaches out with his right arm to locate the sawhorse.

Bear leads Tom through the sawhorse maze along Cortlandt Street.

to the curb. Again the dog could go under the obstacle but the student couldn't. And finally, a series of sawhorses were set up, making a kind of winding maze out of the sidewalk along Cortlandt Street.

Sharon and Bob both took pretty good bops on the first overhanging bar. The dogs were corrected with the leash correction, the bar was tapped out, and the dogs told "No." Then it was reworked.

Tom had some trouble with the second obstacle. After locating it, he gave Bear the correct command, "Forward," but he didn't let Bear decide the best way to take him around. Since the horse extended all the way out to the curb on the right, Bear wanted Tom to *turn* to the right and follow him to the curb. But Tom wanted to *sidestep* to the right around the obstacle, keeping his body facing straight ahead. Bear was correct. By sidestepping, Tom might have stepped off the curb without realizing it and fallen. By turning and following Bear, Bear would be able to stop at the curb and let Tom know it was there. The old "Follow your dog" again.

The maze along Cortlandt was a real "Follow your dog" test. Bear took Tom through the rest of it like a square dancer leading a Grand Right and Left. Then, on the way back along North Division, Bear decided to detour Tom into the pizza parlor. Last Friday, confession; today, pizza. Bear is becoming Tom's spiritual adviser as well as his guide dog. From the smell of cheese and tomatoes, Tom knew right away what had happened. Smell is another sense blind people are much more tuned into than sighted people. It locates the florist, the dry cleaners, the shoe shop, and the pizza parlor.

Bear takes a well-deserved snooze.

EVENING. Lecture. The students were given a strap of leather about the length of a short belt and shown how to wrap it behind the dog's head and over his snout as a muzzle. No one's enthusiastic about the muzzles, but since guide dogs are permitted in public places like buses, trains, airplanes, restaurants, and theaters, owners have the legal right to ask that the dog be muzzled for the sake of other patrons. The students were asked to put the muzzles on the dogs every morning after breakfast for the rest of the week. They can take them off after the van ride to class.

Tomorrow, and for the two days following, the class will be going to White Plains, a city of 50,000 in Westchester County, New York. Unlike Peekskill, the sidewalks are wide and smooth, with a definite flow of traffic on one side and a definite building line on the other. There will be a lot of pedestrians on the sidewalk and traffic in the streets. There may also be a lot of pigeon distractions. A lot of the curbs at the intersections have been cut away for wheelchair access. If the dog runs them (fails to stop), correct him and rework the curb. Remember that when parallel traffic starts going, you start going. Work the dogs with confidence and give them lots of encouragement.

Brenda seems to be feeling pretty low this evening. She says it's just a cold, but I wonder. This is Brenda's very first class as an instructor. She and Don trained Billy's dog Denver for three months for this class, and Denver failed the traffic checks. Guiding Eyes will find Denver a good home, but failures such as this can be rough on the instructors.

LATER. Around 9:30, Caroline and Tom stopped by my room for a few minutes after grooming Buffy and Bear. Caroline was relieved for Billy that Charlie had acted so quickly in retiring Denver, especially since we are going to White Plains tomorrow.

Caroline is now completely enamored of the wondrous Buffy, who has a light and strikingly full coat for a golden retriever, and a somewhat whimsical attitude. Caroline thinks he would make a great spy dog; he would look great in disguises. (He's also an extremely fine guide dog, Caroline.)

Caroline is curious to know how Buffy will react to White Plains tomorrow, to know what he will do. She asks Tom what he thinks Bear will do. With a big smile, Tom answers quick as a wink, "Window-shop. Bear loves to window-shop."

TUESDAY, JUNE 17, WHITE PLAINS, NEW YORK

White Plains

MORNING. Before loading the vans, Don and Brenda checked the dogs for muzzles. Several of the students had forgotten. It almost seems as if the students mind the muzzles more than the dogs do.

We arrived at the side entrance to Saint Matthew's Lutheran Church a little before 9:00 A.M. Saint Matthew's lets Guiding Eyes use a large room on the second floor of the school wing the three days a month they are in White Plains. Students use it as a rest and assembly area and a lunchroom at noontime.

Downtown White Plains is undergoing a major reconstruction of its streets as part of an urban development program. And it's wild! The streets are all torn up, traffic rerouted, parts of Main Street closed altogether, crossings blocked off, heavy, noisy construction machinery all over the place. Charlie scrapped the route planned for the morning and improvised one with Brenda and Don that was reasonably clear. Charlie wanted to get the students underway quickly before the streets got too crowded.

60

In White Plains, New York, construction and obstruction are everywhere.

The morning walks were a bit hectic but without incident. The dogs picked up their pace considerably, which, Charlie told me, is normal when first working a new area. The more familiar they are with a route, the more likely they are to goof off a bit, slow down, look around a lot. But in a new area they are more eager and alert.

AFTERNOON. The plan for the afternoon was a walk down to Macy's, at the end of Main Street, where the students would practice shopping tomorrow. But it became apparent that there were now so many closed streets and obstructions that there was no way to get there. Charlie again improvised routes in a less congested area near the church.

The reason for going to White Plains in the first place was to give the students a chance to work the wider sidewalks and use the increased traffic flow to smooth out their work and gain confidence in their ability to work the dogs in major downtown areas. It's much livelier than Peekskill and it should be easier. But today was a long and frustrating day. And it was hot. Most of the students slept or sat quietly in the vans on the way back to Yorktown.

The new simplified muzzles aren't so bad after all.

Shopping

MORNING. Overnight, the path to Macy's seemed to have opened up magically. There were a couple of tricky spots, but otherwise it looked good.

The students were to walk to Macy's in their usual pairs, enter the store, and spend twenty to thirty minutes freelance shopping. The choice was theirs. Tom wanted to look at portable radios. Dan said that was all right with him, so they set off with Bear and Tucker.

Macy's is a very large department store and difficult to shop without assistance. Tom's outgoing personality and smile work very well for him, and within minutes he and Dan had several offers of assistance. It was early and not too crowded, and a helpful saleswoman had time to take Tom and Dan up to the Stereo Department personally. When they were finished looking, the stereo salesman took Tom and Dan back to the elevator.

Finding the Main Street exit on the first floor proved to be a bit of a challenge. The store was busier now and the salespeople had less time. They'd give directions like "It's down past Men's Shirts and then left," perhaps assuming that Tom and Dan would then tell Bear and Tucker to take them to Men's Shirts.

When Tom and Dan finally met Brenda and Charlie (who in reality were following them all the time they were inside), Tom remarked how difficult it is for blind people to shop in big stores if they don't know their way around. The aisles are usually narrow and wind in and out of merchandise and displays. It is very easy to get lost without assistance.

The dogs seem to like shopping. They usually get quite a lot of attention. The students are encouraged not to let people pet the dogs while they are in harness, working. But

Shopping at Macy's in White Plains. Bear seems to think a watch would be nice.

it is often hard to know. Children, especially, will just run up and hug the dog and then run back to Mommy without the blind person even being aware it happened. The students are also reminded that when they are offered assistance, indoors or on the street, they are to drop the handle and "heel" the dog.

One problem can be pretty persistent. People in stores

are often carrying shopping bags at about the level of the dog's nose. There are a lot of temptations to sniff, and it catches some people by surprise. Some are amused, some don't like it very much. Sniffing is a natural, and important, instinct in a dog, as natural as breathing is to us. The instinct can't be eliminated, but it can be inhibited quite a bit with a mild but sudden leash correction.

AFTERNOON. The White Plains schedule calls for the afternoon to be spent working on obstructions. It seems like all of White Plains is an obstruction at the moment, so just about any route will do.

EVENING. Tom is very tired this evening, and he's a little pale. His blood sugar may be low. But we're all tired.

Tom and Bear return from their shopping spree.

THURSDAY, JUNE 19, WHITE PLAINS

Buses and escalators

MORNING. On the way to White Plains, Ross, one of the students, showed me the way he keeps bills in his wallet. There is no uniform method of folding, each person has his own. Ross leaves singles flat out, fives he folds in half lengthwise, tens in half widthwise, and twenties in quarters. When receiving bills in change, Ross always takes his time and folds the bills before putting them in his wallet. It sometimes slows things down a bit at the cash register, but it is the only safe way.

I am beginning to realize—finally—that there are very few things that blind people can't do as effectively as sighted people. It is mostly a matter of learning new ways of doing things. Sighted people rely on sight so much for receiving information, that they don't realize just how many other ways there are to get the same information. A blind person preparing to cross a street, who is concentrating on what he or she is doing, might well have a more accurate picture of traffic conditions than a sighted person who isn't paying strict attention.

The class exercise this morning was a trip on a White Plains city bus. The students worked the dogs to the downtown area and then took the bus back. The technique: Listen for the bus to stop and the door to open. Listen for people getting off and then on the bus. Work the dog to the bus and up the steps; the first step is usually quite high. Use the harness handle for balance. In some areas blind people can ride public transportation free, in other areas for half fare. Tell the driver where you want to get off, drop the handle, and "heel" the dog to a seat. Let someone else know, as a backup, where you want to get off. Sit down and put the dog under the seat or sit him between your legs as

Brenda gives Bear a push to get him moving up the steps of the bus.

close as possible. Keep the dog out of the aisle and be careful of his tail. Don't let the dog sniff.

When exiting, "heel" the dog to the steps at the front of the bus. Ask the driver where you are in relation to the curb and also in relation to the corner. Ask for specific streets. On the steps pick up the handle—again for balance—and work the dog off the bus. Remember that the last step off is usually a high step. If you travel a bus route regularly, try to make friends with the driver.

Getting off the escalator, Tom has moved too far out in front of Bear. Brenda steps in to see that Bear gets off safely.

Everyone seemed to find it easy. Only the high step up and down was a little difficult. A few passengers seemed a trifle annoyed that it took the students time to get on and off. The newer "kneeling" buses would make getting on and off considerably easier and quicker.

AFTERNOON. This afternoon it was back to Macy's to practice on the escalators. There used to be a rule in guide dog work about never using escalators. They are obviously very tricky and there is a danger of the dog getting a toenail caught in the moving stairs. But now there are many more buildings with escalators and sometimes they can't be avoided. So the rule has been changed to: Never use an escalator unless you absolutely have to.

The technique that Guiding Eyes teaches is: "Heel" the dog, on, "heel" the dog off. It is not necessarily the same technique that other schools teach. But Guiding Eyes feels that by "heeling," using the leash instead of the harness handle, the dog has more freedom to position himself comfortably and will be more relaxed. The technique: Work the dog up onto the metal plate that begins about four feet from the first moving step. Tap out the metal plate with your left foot. Reach forward with your right hand and tap out the handrail. Praise the dog. When ready to step onto the stairs, give the command "Juno, heel" and step forward onto the first step. Make sure the dog remains standing, and don't let him get too far in front of you or he may pull you off.

You will know when you are nearing the bottom or top of the escalator because you will feel the handrail begin to flatten out. As soon as you do, that's your signal to get moving. Tell the dog, "Juno, heel," and pick up your feet and get him moving. Expect a bit of a jolt when you get off.

Most of the dogs were a bit edgy and worried about the escalators, especially on the first ride. They were a little slow and reluctant getting on, and a little too happy getting off. The second ride was smoother for all. I think any one of the students confronted with an escalator on a regular basis could master it, but it is very clear why escalators should never be used if they can be avoided.

The class was finished by 3:30, a little early, and everyone was glad to leave White Plains once and for all. No lecture this evening.

EVENING. Back at Guiding Eyes, it was a warm, sunny evening and light until almost 9:00. I took Tom and Bear for a walk out by the Norway spruce and we talked while Bear rolled around in the grass and then went to sleep.

Tom didn't think White Plains had really smoothed out anyone's teamwork as it was supposed to. They were difficult days—long rides in the van, all the streets torn up, all the obstacles; it wasn't easy. But Tom said he had learned a lot anyway, and his confidence in Bear continues to grow. "Bear knows what he's doing; it's me that makes the mistakes."

I asked Tom if his blood sugar had been low the last day or so; he seemed tired. "A little bit. It's always been hard for me to regulate anyway, but on long days like today in White Plains, when it's so hot, it's even harder to control."

Tom's blood sugar problems are the main symptoms of his diabetes, a disease that occurs when the cells of the pancreas fail to provide the body with a sufficient supply of insulin. Insulin is the hormone which stabilizes and regulates the amount of sugar in the bloodstream. The blood sugar level of diabetics is often highly variable, swinging from abnormally high levels to abnormally low levels and back again. Both extremes are dangerous. If the blood sugar level becomes too high, the blood sugar passes from the bloodstream through the kidneys and into the urine, causing extreme thirst, hunger, weakness, weight loss, and unusually large amounts of urine. If, on the other hand, the blood sugar level becomes too low, the diabetic can become confused, fatigued, and even lose consciousness altogether. Controlling and regulating blood sugar levels through diet and insulin injections are extremely important to the health and well-being of a diabetic.

Tom's diabetes was first discovered when he was six years old. He was living in Germany, where his dad was stationed. Tom came down with a case of German measles, and instead of lasting the usual three or four days, it lasted for more than three weeks. He was thirsty all the time, drinking a lot, urinating a lot, hungry all the time, and getting skinnier and skinnier.

He was put in the Army hospital for almost a week of tests. When it was discovered that he was diabetic, the doctors first thought it might be controlled with diet alone since his pancreas was still producing some insulin. But diet control didn't work and Tom was back in the hospital over Christmas that year while they tried to find the right doses of insulin for daily injection.

Tom didn't really understand what was wrong with him. He thought the insulin shots would stop after he left the hospital. Tom's dad remembers that some days they'd have to hold him down to give him the injections. Other days he wouldn't seem to mind them at all. "I didn't understand why I was getting shots and why I was on such a strict diet, weighing everything. I felt like I was different from everyone else, a freak or something. I'd cry myself to sleep most nights."

And the strict diet made sweets all the more tempting because they were forbidden. Tom would always have to carry something sweet with him in case his blood sugar dropped. It never did, but Tom ate the sweets anyway.

The Kalecs returned to the States that summer, 1963, and his dad was stationed in South Carolina. They lived on the Army base for a while and then bought land and built a house nearby. Tom felt good most of the time and had lots of energy—and kept right on sneaking sweets. He'd save his money and get candy and Cokes with the other kids. When he'd buy a diet soda, the other kids would say, "What are you drinking that diet stuff for?"

"I never told anyone I was a diabetic; I hated the word. I didn't want anyone to know that I was different."

As I guided Tom and Bear back to their room, I asked

Tom if he had had any awareness at all during those years that eating lots of sweets, failing to control his diet, could lead to later complications. "None at all. I just thought I might have a blood sugar reaction and feel sick for a while," he said.

FRIDAY, JUNE 20, PEEKSKILL

The pole

MORNING. There was a gray drizzle at first. This morning the students were given a new route. They were to cross North Division Street for the first time and work a section along Nelson Avenue. Tom and Dan were the first to work the route. They handled it well. Working a new area, Bear and Tucker were extra alert. The crossings, in spite of or because of White Plains, I'm not sure which, are getting straighter and smoother.

Toward the end of the route, as they approached Main Street from North Division, Tom and Bear were in the lead, with Dan and Tucker about ten paces behind. Tucker was straining to catch up with Bear. Brenda was behind Dan helping him "steady" Tucker down. All of a sudden . . . CRASH! Brenda stopped Dan and ran toward Tom. Tom had run into the pole of a No Parking sign and banged his head a good one. There was a cut above his right eye. Even before Brenda reached him, Tom gave Bear a strong left-handed leash correction and then banged the sign with his right hand and shouted "No! No!" at Bear. Tom was surprised at how quickly he had corrected Bear. He had done it instinctively.

Tom didn't think it was Bear's fault. There are metal fire doors placed in the sidewalk right opposite the pole so the sidewalk passage between the doors and the pole is fairly narrow. Bear tries to avoid walking on the metal doors, which

After Tom walked into a No Parking sign, Don checks Tom's fore-head—and Tom reassures Bear that he's okay.

Tom jokingly feels his head to make sure it's still there, but Bear is still worried, almost blocking Tom from the curb.

are often burning hot from the sun. He has taken Tom through this narrow stretch many times before, always safely. Tom thinks that this time he let Bear get too far out in front of him, instead of keeping him back by his side where it is easier to follow Bear more accurately.

Tom insisted it wasn't serious—a little bloody, but not serious. Brenda stayed right by his side all the way back to the lounge. In spite of his bleeding forehead, Tom knelt down and gave Bear a big hug, to reassure him and let him know he was all right. Don tended to Tom's forehead. Tom wanted to know what everyone was so concerned about; after all, he wasn't "the first one to bump into a pole."

"No, that's true," said Joyce. "But you were the first one to get results."

Bill took Tom to the doctor. Bear was left in the lounge with Joe and his dog Tobias. Brenda, who had handled the whole incident very calmly and well, then had her moment of delayed shock and went white.

Bill and Tom returned about forty-five minutes later. Tom had four stitches, covered by a bandage, over his right eye. Tom was in good spirits and decided to test his "Honest Tom" reputation with the other students by pretending amnesia. He went around saying, "Where am I? Who are you?" And Joyce almost fell for it.

Marty Yablonski, Coordinator of Student Admissions, videotaped each of the students this morning as they crossed North James Street. The videotape is kept in the files, and if the student has any difficulties after he gets back home, the instructors can check the videotape to refresh their memories of the student's walk, pace, and general handling of the dog. It might offer some helpful clues.

AFTERNOON. The exercise for the afternoon was freelance shopping. After White Plains, this was easy. The students were old pros already. Tom and Dan didn't have any shopping they wanted to do, so they worked a route near the lounge. As it turned out, it was rather a good thing. Tom looked fine, full of smiles. But all of a sudden he began to feel a little dizzy and started to fall backward. Brenda was right there; she'd been sticking very close to Tom. After steadying him, she insisted that Tom go back to the lounge and rest. He was beginning to get a headache.

Caroline uses the Sonicguide while Orientation and Mobility specialist Marty Yablonski observes.

Caroline used her Sonicguide while working Buffy this afternoon. The Sonicguide—eyeglass frames and a control unit—sends out high frequency sounds imperceptible to the ear. When ultrasound hits an object such as a wall or a tree, it is reflected back to the Sonicguide and is converted into audible sound. The pitch, volume, and quality of the sound all vary according to the density and distance of the object. And if the object is to the side, the sound will be louder in the ear nearest the object.

Caroline has used the Sonicguide for more than three years and did some work with it with her previous dog, Carla, before the dog was retired in 1977. Since then Caroline has used the Sonicguide and the cane for travel and mobility almost exclusively.

When used with a guide dog, the Sonicguide can locate landmarks and interpret obstacles, but it can also interfere with the pace and work of the dog. It's quite popular with guide dog users in Australia, but much less so here. Caroline is uncertain about it, even more so after the walk. But she wants to give it another try.

EVENING. Lecture. Some of the students will be working their dogs in suburban and country areas, college campuses, places where there may be no curbs, no sidewalks, and very little traffic. Always walk on the left-hand side of the street, facing the oncoming traffic. That way the dog can pull you to the side and out of the way more easily if necessary. And you are better able to hear cars coming toward you. Every time you hear a car coming, from either direction, use the "Left, left" command and slap your right leg several times to encourage the dog to stay well over to the left. To a dog a road looks like a wide sidewalk, so he may try weaving and working toward the center. Keep after him. You should be able to feel some kind of build-up of grass, leaves, or gravel, to check that you are far enough to the side. Expect many more distractions, such as squirrels and birds, in the country; don't expect the dog's concentration to be as good.

Tomorrow morning, students will be called to work country routes one at a time, and Don and Brenda will do extra work with those who expect to work country routes frequently.

SATURDAY, JUNE 21, YORKTOWN HEIGHTS

Country routes

MORNING. First day of summer. The country routes mapped out by Guiding Eyes are not casual strolls about the countryside. They are just as precise and prescribed as city routes, but often without the advantages of sidewalks and curbs to mark the all-important intersections, steady traffic flow to aid in direction, and frequent landmarks.

It is essential to make intersections very special to the dogs so that they will learn to stop at each intersection.

Brenda and class supervisor Charlie Mondello take Tom and Bear on their first country walk.

The technique is to fake a stumble and push the harness handle forward, causing the dog to lose balance. This calls the dog's attention to an important spot and in country routes substitutes for the "tap, tap" method of marking curbs, steps, and doors.

After faking the stumble, drop the handle and "heel" the dog back ten or twelve steps, counting the steps. Pick up the handle and give the command, "Hup-up." When you've reworked the intersection or landmark and the dog does not stop, fake another stumble and rework again. It will take some practice.

Tom and Bear managed pretty well. Tom has to be careful about faking too hard a stumble or Bear gets worried about him and stops too far from the intersection. Bear is also still crossing his body in front of Tom at intersections to protect him, and this makes proper body alignment a bit difficult for Tom. And like most of the dogs, Bear at first tends to work toward the middle of the road when there is no traffic. Tom has to keep reminding Bear, "Left, left."

Bear just can't seem to get close enough to Tom.

AFTERNOON. There was a cookout at lunchtime; the second week of training is just about over. Nolan has been chewing a lot on his bandaged leg and so a rather ingenious bucket was devised to put around his head. Now "Old Buckethead," as we affectionately call him, can't chew. But it didn't keep him from stealing an ice cream cone that Anita tried to give Sue. Nolan just reached over and grabbed it in one bite. And later, Tucker managed to get a sandwich that Dan had left on the desk in his room. Guide dogs will be dogs first.

At the 4:00 P.M. "park," Tom was telling Bear to "get busy" when Brenda noticed that Tom was parking Dolly not Bear. That came as quite a surprise to Tom. He'd been asleep when the call to park came over the speaker and he'd gotten up and called Bear to come. But obviously it was his roommate Billy's dog that had come, and Tom just put the leash on her and took her out. Tom took quite a lot of teasing for that one.

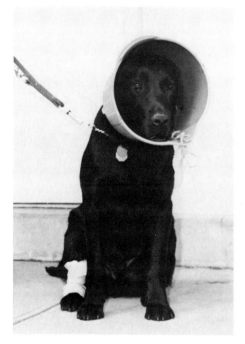

Nolan wears a bucket on his head to prevent him from chewing his bandage.

EVENING. Tom and Bear and I picked up some soda and cookies from the lounge and sat outside and talked. He told me that in 1967, when he was eleven years old, his dad was sent to Vietnam for a year. Tom was put in the hospital for a few days to learn how to give himself his insulin injections, now that he was to be the "man around the house."

In 1968, after his tour of duty in Vietnam was over, Tom's dad asked to be stationed in Japan. Tom finally got to meet his grandparents on his mother's side of the family. Tom loved Japan, and the family stayed there for the next five years.

During his last year in Japan, Tom got a job as part of the Army's "summer hire" program. He and another boy, Billy, had charge of cleaning up the teen club. They'd get their work done quickly and have a lot of time left over to talk. By the end of the summer they were good friends. When it came time to return to the United States in the summer of 1973, Tom didn't want to leave. "That's one thing about the Army! You make good friends, and then you leave and never see them again," he said.

Back in South Carolina, Tom spent a lonely and boring senior year in high school. All his friends had moved while he was in Japan, and the few who were still around had become strangers. During the second quarter, Tom got a job at the canteen in the Army hospital. He liked the job and made a lot of friends around the hospital. He kept the job all during that summer and through his freshman year at the University of South Carolina. It was toward the end of his freshman year that Tom first started having headaches. He thought he'd been working too hard. So toward the end of that summer, 1975, he decided to relax for a couple of weeks and went along with the family to visit his grandparents in Iowa.

One afternoon, Tom and his younger brother Mike were downstairs in the basement when Tom realized that he couldn't see the numbers on the calendar across the room, even though Mike was able to read them all easily. Next he noticed that the road signs were all fuzzy, when he drove his cousins to the movies. Since one of his cousins wore glasses, he borrowed a pair from her and was able to see more clearly with them. He thought he'd better get his eyes checked when he got back home.

The daily headaches had eased while Tom was in Iowa, but when he went back to work the headaches came back, which convinced him all the more that they were from tension. Tom made an appointment with the optometrist and found his vision to be a very poor 20/60 in both eyes. The optometrist was concerned about all the "junk" in back of Tom's eyes and insisted Tom make an appointment with the ophthalmologist.

I interrupted Tom to ask if still no one had told him that diabetes could potentially lead to blindness, kidney failure, and circulation problems in the legs, and that poor diet control could hasten the onset of such problems. "No," he said. "The doctors and my parents told me that if I didn't take care of myself I wouldn't live very long, but I didn't know what they meant. And they told me always to take care of my legs, but I wasn't sure what that meant either."

The headaches continued to get worse. Tom started losing his temper all the time. "If a door was hard to open, I'd kick it. I got mad at my mom a lot. I was starting to be someone else—a wild man. The people I worked with just couldn't believe it was me. And my vision fluctuated every day."

Then it was discovered that Tom's blood pressure was extremely high. Tom was put on medication, which would bring his pressure down at first, but then it would shoot right back up. They had to keep doubling the medication, and the side effects were disastrous. Tom couldn't concentrate and he couldn't study. He was tired all the time and would fall asleep in class. His grades dropped; Tom was flunking, and the doctors weren't really getting anywhere with the blood pressure.

Then one morning in early November, while he was cooking his breakfast, Tom heard a "pop" and felt a burning in his left eye. At first he thought maybe he had gotten salt or pepper in it, but when he closed his right eye and looked through his left, everything was red. He drove to the hospital and the ophthalmologist examined the eye. "Eye hemorrhages!" Tiny blood vessels in the back of his eye had popped and Tom was looking through blood.

Tom was put in the hospital. After three or four days of bed rest and eye drops, the blood that was blocking his vision settled downwards, restoring sight to his left eye. He could see again.

SUNDAY, JUNE 22, YORKTOWN HEIGHTS

The Sonicguide

MORNING. Country walks were much smoother this morning. Bear did very well at remembering the intersections Tom marked by faking stumbles yesterday, and he kept well to the left most of the time.

Tom and Dan went to church this morning and left the dogs on bedchains in their rooms. Since Bear likes to chew, Tom was careful about leaving things well out of his reach. But he came back to find that Bear had managed to chew up a bar of soap, a bottle of cologne, and a box of alcohol pads that Tom had left on his desk. Bear can reach quite a bit farther on the bedchain than Tom had realized. Bear is now very lonely without Tom.

NOON. Beginning with lunch this noon, and at every meal from now on, students sharing rooms are to alternate leaving

I tried to hide down a dirt side road to get a picture of Tom and Bear on this morning's country walk, but Bear was very alert and spotted me.

Tom checks out Bear's new custom-fitted handle and harness.

their dogs on the bedchain during meals, to get the dogs used to being left alone once in a while.

EVENING. New harnesses and custom-fitted handles were given to each of the students, based on the size and weight of the dog and the student's arm length.

Caroline asked everyone who was interested in trying her Sonicguide to meet in the Campbell Lounge. Caroline let each of us try the unit. When it was my turn, I stood about fifteen feet from a wall. The sound, at that distance, was very high pitched, like a soprano voice sustaining a high note. As I approached the wall, the pitch dropped until it was like a low hum, at which point I could reach out and touch the wall.

Then Caroline had me walk down a hallway, scanning my head left and right as I walked. As the walls were quite close, the pitch was low. But all of a sudden the pitch of the tone shot up, which meant no more wall! It was either an intersection or a doorway. By scanning the head a bit more, it was easy to determine that it was a doorway. Then Caroline had me stand in front of the stairs up to the dining room. This time the sound was more like a chord than a single tone, suggesting, correctly, that the object was various distances in front of me. The whole experience was, for me at least, like listening to the soundtrack of a science fiction movie. With considerable practice, Sonicguide users can learn to distinguish subtleties of sound and thereby know a great deal about what is around them at any given moment.

However, I can also see how easy it would be to become very absorbed in hearing what is around you and how that could interfere with the pace and work of the dog. When working with a Sonicguide and a dog, you have to learn to process the sounds considerably faster than you would using it with a cane. But clearly it can be done . . . especially by the more experienced.

LATER. Later in the evening, Tom and Bear dropped by my room to ask about Caroline's demonstration of the Sonicguide. Tom had intended to go to it too but had fallen asleep on his bed after dinner. He felt wide awake now and offered to go on with his story.

After that first hemorrhage in the left eye, and three weeks in the hospital for bed rest and another attempt to better control his diabetes, Tom thought things were clearing up, except for the fact that he had fallen pretty far behind in school. He went back to a normal routine of school and work.

But then, in the beginning of January, while working at the canteen one Saturday, he had another hemorrhage in the left eye. This time it was a massive one. The vision in his left eye was completely blocked. Tom could see the blood in his eye flowing *up*. (It was actually flowing down through the eye, but because the brain inverts the image, it appeared to Tom to be flowing up.) "If I'd close my right eye, everything would be black. I started to worry."

Three weeks later Tom was sent to an ophthalmologist in Atlanta who specialized in the effects of diabetes on the eyes. In diabetics who develop eye problems (and not all do), tiny blood vessels grow like weeds in the back of the eye, grabbing hold of the retina and squeezing it. The tiny blood vessels are very fragile; when they break, blood leaks out, blocking the vision. Tom's retina was badly crushed and too far gone to be treated with the modern laser techniques.

From the doctor's report, which Tom later read:

As regards the eyes:
Left eye: Hand motions only. There is nothing we can do about the left eye now except to hope that the vitreous hemorrhages will go ahead and clear up.
Right eye: 20/40. Fibrosis. Now showing serious signs of diabetic retinopathy, many small hemorrhages.

86

Tom also showed severe kidney problems, and the doctor's report concluded: "Very obviously this young man is in severe trouble both systemically and ocularly from his diabetes."

Tom quit school; there was no way he could go on. In March the Army ophthalmologist recorded: "Left eye possibly clearing. Vision in right eye variable." Tom had a number of insulin reactions in April and by the end of May was back in the hopsital for "diabetic control, hypertension, headaches, decreased kidney function, and proliferous eye hemorrhages in the right eye."

The Army ophthalmologist finally told Tom what he had suspected but couldn't admit since he read the Atlanta report: he was going blind. He told the doctor, "The day I go blind is the day I'm going to die." "I didn't believe him. I shut it out of my mind. I kept saying my vision wasn't going to get worse . . . and it got worse. As long as I could get around and see a little bit, I refused to believe it."

Tom quit his job at the canteen and had to stop driving. "That's when I realized I just couldn't go wherever I wanted to go; I had to depend on someone, I hated that." And for two weeks straight he couldn't sleep. "I was afraid if I fell asleep I might wake up and not be able to see anymore."

About that time, Tom's friend from Japan, Billy, came to South Carolina. Billy's dad had retired from the Army and decided to live in Columbia. Billy started visiting Tom and tried to get him out of the house. Most of Tom's other friends had slowly stopped coming by. "They were afraid. They didn't know what to say to me." Billy was different. He understood. He knew what it was to face a big problem. Billy had cystic fibrosis and, at best, had only a few more years to live. Tom didn't have to explain to Billy how he felt. There was a deeper communion between them.

Billy got a job in electronics and so was able to stop by less frequently. "In a way, I was mad at him; he was doing something. There I was just lying in bed, mostly in silence, looking forward to the nights when it was okay to try to sleep. And there was Billy, who knew about his cystic fibrosis, who knew he was dying; he had a job."

Slowly, over the months ahead, Tom's right eye got worse, and so did his physical condition. By April of 1977, Tom's stomach had backed up and he was dehydrated, nauseous; he was treated with an experimental drug. And they found glaucoma in his left eye. "I blamed it all on myself, not taking good care of myself. Some doctors say it probably would have happened anyway, but I still think it was my fault. At the very least, I hurried it up."

And it was then that Tom first heard about the Commission for the Blind. "But I hated the word blind. I didn't want anyone to know. Billy kept encouraging me: 'Go to the Commission; go, go, go.'" Finally, in January of 1978, Tom went to the Commission . . . and only stayed a half day. "I didn't like it. I wasn't prepared. I called my mom to come get me and went home. Back to bed. It takes time to lose one hope and find another."

MONDAY, JUNE 23, PEEKSKILL

"Drop-off"

MORNING. Revolving Doors. The student makes certain that the revolving door is stopped. He drops the harness handle and "heels" the dog to his right side, one of the few, if not the only, times in guide dog work when the dog is on the right. The student steps into the door and uses his left heel to block the door from moving until both the student and the dog are safely positioned in the door, being especially careful that the dog's tail doesn't get caught.

Revolving doors are not easy to work with a dog and,

Brenda shows Tom how to use his left heel to block a revolving door from moving until he gets Bear safely inside.

like escalators, are to be avoided whenever possible. It's a slow procedure and is especially difficult at crowded and busy times.

It seemed a little hard for most of the students to get back into harness this morning. There's a bit of a nervous edge in the air; most of the students are expecting, and wondering about, a surprise "drop-off" exercise this afternoon.

AFTERNOON. Don and Brenda drove the students into Peekskill by a different route, winding through some of the back streets. By then the students were sure what was up. Without the students realizing where they were, the vans parked along a section of the Nelson Avenue route they worked last Friday. The challenge to the students was to find out where they were and work their way back to the lounge.

Charlie reminded them to stick to busy streets where there were stores, traffic, and pedestrians to assist them if they got lost. At five-minute intervals, Don and Brenda walked each student down to the first intersection and wished them luck.

Tom and Bear, as usual, were one of the first teams off. As soon as Tom crossed the first intersection he heard voices inside a shop and stopped in to ask directions. He learned immediately where he was: on North Division Street. Farther along the smell of pizza assured him, and Bear, that they were right, and at intersections he asked pedestrians to verify his direction. Tom's outgoing personality is a big help to him in situations like this.

Tom had no difficulty finding his way back to the lounge. But crossing two of the intersections, Tom and Bear veered considerably off to the left and as a result had to take seven or eight sidesteps to the right to get back on the sidewalk. Since Tom was one of the first to complete the drop off, he asked an Orientation and Mobility intern who was observing the training at Guiding Eyes to check his turns and body alignment.

Part of the problem was that Bear was continuing to cross his body in front of Tom at intersections and curbs to protect him. That pleased Tom, although he knew it was wrong to let him do it. Instead of correcting Bear, Tom would compensate by turning his body into Bear, toward the left, when starting to cross. That's what was often causing them to veer to the left.

90

At the drop-off point, guide dog teams wait their turn to work their way back to the lounge.

During the drop-off exercise, Tom stops almost immediately to ask for directions.

It "clicked" in Tom's head: too much protection creates as many problems as too little. He realized that from listening to the traffic flow and making certain that he maintained his straight ahead position coming into the curb, he then could make certain that Bear was aligned alongside his body and also facing directly ahead. That solved the problem. Tom realized that it was *his* responsibility to be aligned in the right direction and that Bear was not a magic dog who would always go straight, even if Tom didn't.

EVENING. Before the evening lecture, Caroline summed up almost everyone's feelings about the drop-off exercise: "That is the kind of lesson that gives you faith in your dog." The students were all given permanent choke chains for the dogs with a metal tag that had Guiding Eyes' address and phone number stamped on it.

Tomorrow, a night walk in Mount Kisco.

TUESDAY, JUNE 24, MOUNT KISCO, NEW YORK

Night Walk

MORNING. On the way to Mount Kisco this morning to go over the route of the night walk, there was quite a bit of discussion about a story that had appeared in the *Daily News* yesterday. A young blind musician whose thirteen-year-old guide dog had died last week had been refused a replacement dog by Guiding Eyes because the musician had been giving frequent sidewalk performances of his music using a casette recorder. Guiding Eyes considered this a form of begging.

The discussion was lively. Some of the students were sympathetic with the young musician's problems trying to get along in New York. Others looked on what he was doing

The night walk.

quite flatly and unsympathetically as begging. When I asked
how they felt about Guiding Eyes refusing the musician a
dog, they all agreed with and supported Guiding Eyes' position. Since everyone had signed a pledge not to beg, they
viewed the musician's street corner performances as a viola-
tion of that pledge. Further, most blind people are troubled
enough by the image that the public has of them as second-
class citizens who have to be led around. Anything that in
any way could be construed as begging would be very dam-
aging to the public image of all blind guide dog users. All
of these students are struggling very hard to be independent
and to prove to the public, and in many instances even to

their own families, that they can be. To them, any form of begging strikes a blow at their self-image, pride, and spirit of independence.

The night route is a large triangle around the center of Mount Kisco. The route was talked over with the students. They were told that there were several wheelchair ramps and driveways that the dogs should not be allowed to over-run.

Since the route is all right turns today, Tom had a good chance to practice right turns with Bear. And he found the answer to another of his problems. When he'd give Bear the command "Bear, right," he'd expect Bear to make a perfect right turn. Today Tom realized it was up to him to make sure that he was properly and squarely aligned and that *he* make an accurate 90° turn so that he was guiding Bear. Bear knows what "right" is; 90° is another matter. Tom had been expecting too much of Bear again. But he's got it now, and the right turns are noticeably smoother.

There were no problems with the route, although some of the dogs needed to be corrected several times at first for running the wheelchair ramps.

NOON. At noontime the dogs were taken to the kennels to get booster rabies and distemper shots. After lunch, a photographer came to take a class picture and individual shots of each of the students and their dogs for their Guiding Eyes identification cards and also for their personal use. The students were given medical papers for their dogs, containing the dogs' birth dates. Bear was born October 16, 1978, a few months after Tom went blind. Something ends, something else begins. . .

EARLY EVENING. Several of the students whose level of work was considered satisfactory and safe by the instructors were given the option of going home on Sunday, a few days

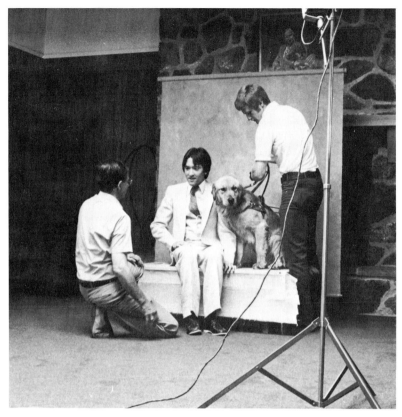

Don helps Tom and Bear pose for their class picture.

early. Anita, Howard, and Joe have decided to leave.

Guiding Eyes veterinarian Dr. Remsen talked to the students in the Campbell Lounge about the importance of taking the dogs to veterinarians for regular checkups. Guide dogs are working dogs. And even under the best of circumstances it is stressful work. Guide dogs are under a great deal more daily stress than family pets and are therefore more susceptible to disease. They should be given a complete physical checkup at least twice a year.

Dr. Remsen answered questions about ears, skin, fleas, ticks, worms, grooming, and feeding, and gave advice about remembering to clean out the dog's feet frequently to prevent the dog from doing it by chewing and irritating the paw. Dr. Remsen advised them to keep the dogs lean. "If obesity is bad for people, it's a disaster in a dog. It places a tremendous strain on the hind legs and the heart." There is no doubt about it, a guide dog is a big responsibility. Any dog requires attention and care, guide dogs especially so. These students take the responsibility readily, but I can see that it is a responsibility that not every blind person would want to take or would be able to handle.

LATER. Back in Mt. Kisco before starting the night walk, Don told the class that dogs can't see as well at night. They see lots of shadows, so don't be surprised if they seem a little suspicious at times or even growl a little. They might also react a bit to oncoming headlights.

Most of the dogs set a good fast pace. A few of the students were confused at first. The vans were parked farther down the block than they had been that morning. In the morning the students had to cross two driveways to get to the first intersection. In the evening they only had to cross one, and a few thought the intersection was the second driveway. Tom, however, was not counting driveways but was listening to the traffic flow, so he easily recognized the second curb as the intersection, not a driveway.

Tomorrow, the Bronx!

WEDNESDAY, JUNE 25, THE BRONX, NEW YORK

Subways

MORNING AND AFTERNOON. It must have been almost 90° by the time we arrived at the Fordham Methodist Church, which was to be our home base today. And the day got hotter and hotter with every minute. It was hard

96

Subways aren't too bad . . . when they're not crowded.

to think about anything else. By late morning the streets were very crowded. It was not an easy day for either the students or the dogs.

In the morning, Don and Brenda took each student, one at a time, on a subway trip. They worked the dogs from the church to Fordham Road, entered the subway, got on the train, rode three stops, got off, waited for the train back to Fordham Road, and worked the dogs back to the church.

Subways take quite a bit of maneuvering, even for sighted people. And there's a lot of noise. I was really surprised at how calmly most of the dogs handled it. For the students, the special instructions for the subway included standing safely back from the edge of the platform, moving quickly once the subway doors open, making sure of the first step, a long step (possibly a step up or down if the platform and train aren't quite level), and waiting for the train to pull out, after getting off, before trying to orient themselves.

In the afternoon any students who would be using subways frequently were taken on a second trip. The others worked a street route around the Fordham Road area. Joyce stumbled and fell getting into the subway. She slid her foot forward instead of stepping up, and tripped over the doorway. She was a bit shaken up but otherwise okay.

Tucker was walking fast and pulling Dan along, not responding to Dan's "steady" commands. So Dan gave Tucker a good leash correction, which effectively got Tucker's attention. A woman who was watching yelled at Dan, "You're mean, mister, you're mean." People simply don't understand about leash corrections. But it was interesting that when the woman turned back to her little boy and saw that he had gotten ice cream on his shirt, she hauled off and gave him a good smack. I was tempted to yell back, "You're the mean one, lady."

By the middle of the afternoon the streets were crowded and it was unbearably hot, too hot to concentrate. Bear found another line for Tom to get into, this time for a bus. The sidewalks were so hot that the dogs kept moving around and picking up their feet. Back at the church Brenda and Don carefully checked each dog's paws for any signs of irritation or cuts.

Nolan, whom everyone thought was resting quietly after a second trip on the subway with Sharon, made a sudden, sneaky break for the church door; fortunately, Brenda intercepted him. But we all agreed with Nolan: it was time to go home.

In spite of the air conditioning it was too hot to sleep in the vans going back up to Yorktown Heights. No one had much to say.

THURSDAY, JUNE 26

Renewal

MORNING. On the way to Peekskill this morning Eileen mentioned that she'd had a funny dream last night that must have been prompted by the discussion we'd all had about begging. Eileen dreamed that she had been using Indy to pick out cute boys, and that Geoff Lock had found out about it and wanted to take Indy away from her.

The morning in Peekskill was spent free-lancing, working on individual problems. The work is really beginning to smooth out now for the class. The students seem to have the basics of guide dog work down pretty well and are able to concentrate more on the subtleties. It usually takes about six months before a student and a dog really become a strong, well-attuned, smooth team. It's mostly now a matter of continuing to work and practice together.

Today, Tom finally realized the problem that he'd been having with his left turns. After giving the command "Bear,

A picnic at Ward Pound Ridge Reservation.

left," he hadn't been pulling Bear back out of the way but had been turning his body left into Bear's, making an accurate 90° turn difficult to align. By pulling Bear back out of the way *before* he turns his body, it is much easier for Tom to make an accurate turn.

AFTERNOON. Ward Pound Ridge Reservation, Cross River, New York. A cookout and afternoon of relaxation was planned. The students seemed content just to sit at first. It's been almost three weeks now of long, hard days with little time for relaxation or release. In the open but private seclusion of the park, spirits began to rise.

The smell of barbecued hamburgers and hot dogs whetted appetites, and most of the students ate three or four. Bob claimed to be student champion with a total of sixteen. The students put the dogs on their long leashes and began to explore the area and play. Tom wrestled with Bear. Anita

Marty challenges Bear for the stick, but Bear has the upper jaw.

danced around the open field with her dog Sue, whose energy seems boundless. Joyce and Billy and Joe and Bob and Sharon found the swings and challenged each other to see who could swing the highest. The dogs found sticks and challenged each other for possession of them. Bear was smart. He would watch the other dogs play fight over a stick and then he'd sneak up and grab it when one of them wasn't looking. With Indy he just patiently waited until Indy had to relax her jaw for a second to get a better grip on the stick, and then he pulled it way. Bear was clearly King of the Stick.

Don and Bill found a long vine in the woods and the students challenged each other, and the instructors, to a tug of war, while the dogs were all tied to one of the tables, barking them on. All except Bear, that is, who quietly chewed right through his leash and walked over and sat down by Tom. We were so absorbed in the tug of war that we didn't realize at first that he was loose.

It was a joyous afternoon, a celebration. The realization that "we've done it, we've made it, we've come through" was everywhere and the students left the park feeling renewed and at least ten feet tall.

EVENING. Night walk. Mount Kisco. The mood of celebration continued. We all had ice cream in Mount Kisco before the second night walk, which all of the students breezed through confidently. Bear saw a line at the movie theater, hesitated a moment, and then took Tom around it—the first time he's passed up an opportunity to get in a line.

LATER. It was after 10:00 when we returned to Guiding Eyes. Tom was still feeling elated and was happy to talk for a while.

After Tom's first attempt, in January of 1978, at going to the Commission for the Blind, and staying only half a

King of the Stick.

day, he went back to living in bed. "To go to the Commission for the Blind is to admit you accept your blindness, that you're not depressed, and that you're ready to make something out of your life. I wasn't ready. And I still had a little sight left."

Tom locked himself in his room, slept all day and lay awake all night. Time was all confused in his mind. His friend Billy came to see him as often as he could and would try to get

Tom out of the house to a movie. In June his sister, Nina, took him to California to visit some of his friends from Japan. He told his friends, "I'm retired. I don't have to work, I'm medically retired." His friends didn't know what to say, and one later admitted to him that after he had left, she broke down and cried. Tom decided, "If I'm going to make my friends depressed and sad like that, I won't visit anyone anymore. I'll stay in my room."

In August, when his parents asked him what he wanted for his birthday, he said, "Why don't you just buy me a coffin and I'll just use it as a bed. I'm going to die anyway so I'll just make some use out of it now." By then Tom had lost his sight completely and blindness so terrified him that he just wanted to die. It had taken Tom a long time to handle the feeling of being "different" because he was a diabetic. Now blindness was making him "different" again. The word "blind" made him sick to his stomach. "When I was sighted, I avoided blind people. If I saw a blind person coming down the street, I'd make sure he didn't come across my path because I wouldn't know how to act, or know what to say." And now that he was blind, he was sure that people would feel that way about him.

His friend Billy was the one person with whom Tom felt comfortable. Billy didn't pay any attention at all to his blindness, except to urge him to go back to the Commission. Then, early in 1979, Billy came down with a head cold that led to pneumonia and a lung infection. He was given steroids and finally, ironically, became diabetic for a while himself. Billy didn't want Tom to come to the hospital, so Tom wrote him letters and sent him cards. And he'd call Billy's family every day to see how he was doing. "Most of the time he had gotten worse."

On the morning of March 21, Tom got up as usual, ate his breakfast as usual, and went back to bed as usual, around 7:30 A.M. An hour or so later, about 8:30 A.M., the alarm

104

clock wakened him from a dream. "I just saw four words in the dream: 'I love you. Bill.' I didn't understand what it meant."

Later that morning, around 11:00, Billy's dad called to say that Billy had died at 8:30 that morning. The message in Tom's dream had been good-bye. "I actually believe he was telling me good-bye."

Tom's family took him to Billy's funeral. All the depression and anger and rage finally began to pour out. "I just cried and cried and cried. I cried it all out. Billy had been really sick, coughing all the time, spitting up blood. But he never gave up. He was full of life until the day he died. And here I was wasting away in a room, just rotting to death. I'm giving up. Billy didn't give up. Lots of blind people make it. Why can't I? Billy was always encouraging me."

At first Tom just thought about it. As he said before, "It takes time to lose one hope and find another." He started going back to his church and talking to the priests. His grandmother in Japan sent him a short folding cane. He tried it, without knowing anything about using it, when he thought no one was around. He still didn't want people to know he was blind, didn't want to admit that he was beginning at last to accept it. But he couldn't fool the kids. "Why are you blinking your eyes? Why are you feeling your hands all over the place?" And his little brother Ronald would say, "Oh, he's blind!" "That would make my heart just jump out of my throat."

But he did begin to visit people. The neighbors had a new baby and he took them a present. They'd been living next door for over a year and he'd never met them. When he explained who he was, they were surprised. They thought he was living in an apartment somewhere. "No, I've been hiding in my bed. But I've come out, and it's about time."

Tom decided that he wanted a dog, a guide dog. That became his goal. He knew that he would need Orientation and Mobility training with the cane first, so toward the end of November he went back to the South Carolina Commission for the Blind. But living and going to school at the Commission was a dramatic change in daily exercise compared to lying around in bed. And it took several weeks to regulate his insulin shots and control his reactions. With the Christmas holiday vacation, it wasn't really until January that Tom began his training at the Commission in earnest. And now, six months later, he's reached that first goal. He has Bear. "Bear and I are a team now. We're one."

Tom and Bear.

A reaction

MORNING. After breakfast this morning, I asked Caroline if she thought that many other people who go blind had experiences like Tom's. Caroline has been blind longer than the other students, has worked as a teacher and counselor, and is now working on her doctoral thesis. (And, incidentally, she's taking the train to Albany this afternoon, where to-night she will receive Albany's "Blind Woman of the Year Award.")

Caroline said that people going blind often follow similar behavioral patterns and responses as people who learn they are slowly dying. First, the denial and the isolation, the ina-bility to face the facts. "No, it's not true; it's not happening to me." Then the anger. "Why me?" The anger is turned on everyone. Everyone else is resented and envied. Then depression, the deep sense of loss. And finally, for some, acceptance. Tom's was, it seems, a long and universal jour-ney.

It was very hot in Peekskill this morning and some of the magical mood of yesterday was gone. Caroline and Bob got into an argument in the lounge and Ross took a bit of teasing about not participating in the tug of war yesterday. In class Bear is nervous and cautious of narrow passageways or clearances. I imagine he still remembers the pole. Tom had to correct him three times for bumping him lightly into overhanging tree branches.

AFTERNOON. Hotter still. Bill and Don set up the saw-horses and overhanging obstacle again for more practice. Tom and Bear did fairly well with the first one, the overhang, but completely messed up the sawhorses. Tom got confused and Bear got worried. Going down North James, Bear tried

107

Left: Bear stops to warn Tom of an obstacle. Center: Tom "hup-ups" Bear to bring him a little closer—and Bear brings him too close!

Right: Tom taps out the overhanging obstacle with his right hand and tells Bear, "No!"

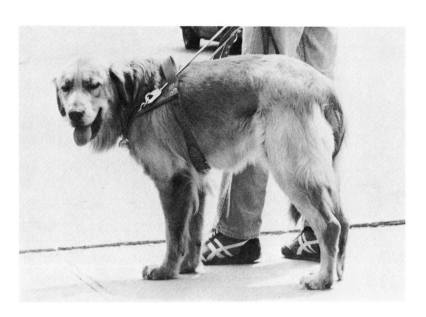

Bear is really worried about Tom here; he has his tail tucked way under his legs.

Brenda gives Tom instant glucose to help bring his blood sugar level up quickly.

to turn in a driveway, and by the time they reached the corner of Main, Tom was pale. He was having a reaction. Brenda had Tom put the harness handle down, to ease Bear of the responsibility, and then gave Tom a tube of instant glucose, which brought his blood sugar level back up within minutes.

Looking back, the reaction obviously had started back at the obstacles. Tom hadn't said anything because he had thought he could handle it. But very hot weather is an additional stress and adds to the body's demand for sugar. Tom realizes now that when he gets confused he passes that confusion on to Bear. Also, the sidewalks were hot enough to be bothering Bear's feet, another distraction. Again Tom has expected too much of Bear. *He* has to know what he's doing, and what Bear is doing, at all times.

After he recovered, Tom wanted to do it all over again. "This time we'll do it right." Charlie, wisely, decided Tom had done enough for today. Bill took Tom to have his stitches removed; the cut from the pole had healed nicely.

EVENING. The lecture this evening was about going home. Anita, Howard, and Joe will be leaving Sunday. It's almost time. The students are advised to give the dogs plenty of time to adjust to all the new situations and surroundings very slowly. At the airport or at home, they should meet people one at a time. The students should remember to take off the harness first, before meeting anyone, and, one at a time, have each person squat down, so as not to overwhelm the dog, and let the dog sniff and get acquainted.

The dogs should meet other family pets, especially other dogs, on neutral ground outside and away from the house; it will help avoid jealousy and turf protection squabbles. Then take them into the house together. Adjustments will take time.

The first days at home the dogs should be "heeled" at

all times in the house and let loose in one room at a time. The dogs should be worked only a short time in a small quiet area where there is not too much stress or pressure. Use only mild corrections. Slowly increase the routes and the areas of traffic a little each day.

When learning a route, work first with a sighted guide, "heeling" the dog and stopping for explanations of intersections, landmarks, and obstacles. Even though the dog is "heeling" and not, therefore, responsible for working, the dog must always stop and sit at every curb or stair. Always. At no time is it ever acceptable for the dog to run a curb or a stair, even when on the leash.

Tomorrrow is Puppy Raisers Day at Guiding Eyes, the day when the 4-H families who raised the dogs until they were a year old come to meet the students. The students have been waiting for this day with great anticipation. They know almost nothing about the backgrounds of their dogs, these creatures who have become so much a part of their lives and will be for years ahead. Tomorrow is the day to ask all the questions they've been storing up.

LATER. The dogs are all being groomed to within an inch of their lives tonight.

Puppy Raisers Day

MORNING. The excitement began a little before 10:00 as the first families began to arrive. Some of them drove hundreds of miles to get here. There were lots of young people and kids. The dogs are raised by 4-H families until they're a year old, helping to assure Guiding Eyes that the dogs are used to people and children and generally well socialized before they are trained. At the age of one year, the dogs are returned to Guiding Eyes for an evaluation. If they pass, they are given three months of training by instructors like Don and Brenda and are then assigned to a class. It is a challenging experience to raise a puppy for a year and then give it up to someone else. Some families have raised eight or nine dogs for Guiding Eyes over the years. Today is a kind of graduation for the dogs, the students, the puppy raisers, and the instructors.

Since the dogs would more than likely become very excited if they caught sight of their former families, the students were asked to remain in their rooms with the dogs until called. One by one, Don and Brenda took each of their students on a country route walk. The family was invited to follow along about twenty yards behind so as not to attract the attention of the dog during the walk. At the end, back by the fountain outside the lounge, the students and families were finally introduced and the dogs went a little crazy. Then the play and the talk and the questions began.

At noontime, while the students parked the dogs, the puppy raisers were shown the kennel, which houses about ninety dogs, and the construction site of the new kennel, which will eventually house ninety more dogs. Those who wanted to went with Jim Maginnis, Breeding Farm Supervisor, to see the puppy farm where the dogs are bred, whelped,

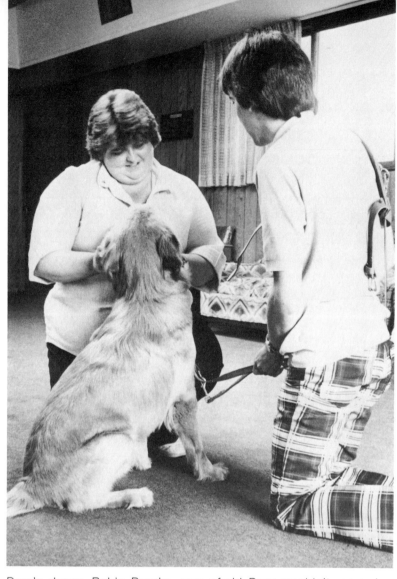

Bear's donor, Robin Brooks, was afraid Bear wouldn't remember her. He did.

weaned, and tested. These are all valuable dogs, carefully bred, lovingly raised, and highly trained.

Bear, as it turns out, was not like the majority of others, a Guiding Eyes–bred puppy. He was donated by a young woman from a suburb of Buffalo, Robin Brooks. Today Robin and a friend who breed and raise golden retrievers drove nine hours straight through from Buffalo just to be here.

It meant a great deal to Robin to see Bear and his new master, as we learned when she told us Bear's story.

It began almost two years ago, thousands of miles away in Anchorage, Alaska, at Lynda Reddington's Reddigold Goldens kennels. Lynda wrote:

Bear's life began October 16, 1978. He was born very early one crisp morning in Anchorage, Alaska. Little did he know as he lay cuddled in the warmth of his mother, Champion Reddigold's Can't Miss, and his three sisters and five brothers, that his path would cross that of a nice young man's named Tom.

Bear's father, Champion Alderbrooke's Bojangles, and his grandfather, Champion Beckwith's North Wind, were the original members of the first Alaskan Golden Retriever Three-Dog Sled Team.

Bear was your basic fuzzy, cute, golden retriever puppy and led a very normal life, consisting of eating, playing, and growing. His most unique trait was his tail. When the spirit moved him, his tail would go straight up in the air. And, oh, what a gay tail it was!

We started our behavioral testing at five weeks of age. As I recall from my notes, Bear didn't score a perfect mark on his tests but he did show an unusual trait for courage, a keen sense of awareness of his surroundings, and a very stable disposition, seeming undisturbed by strange objects or weird noises. However, he did on occasion charge off from a test to investigate a leg of a chair or have a nip n' tug on the foot of the tester!

The day I put Bear on the plane to Robin, I never dreamed or could have known that Bear would become so special: guiding eyes for the blind.

Neither did Robin, who had high hopes for Bear as a show dog and eventually as a stud dog for her BrookLea Kennels. The plane from Alaska missed the connecting flight to Buffalo in Chicago and Bear was held over six hours. The crate finally arrived later that evening. On the top it was labelled:

Above: Bear's mother, Champion Reddigold's Can't Miss. Bear is somewhere in there, and just about a week old. Below: Bear is the puppy in the middle, at five weeks. Courtesy of Lynda Reddington

"Hello. My name is Fella. Please take care of me and deliver me to Robin Brooks."

Robin was nervous; she couldn't see in the crate. When she opened the door, out jumped Bear, not at all shaken up by the ride. He was a little "fluffball" that wouldn't hold still all the way home in the car. "We tried calling him Fella for a few days, but it just didn't fit him. Finally, someone in the family said he looked like a big teddy bear with all his soft puppy coat and his wonderful broad head, so we just started calling him Bear. It was a perfect name for him."

Bear continued to carry his tail straight up in the air until he was almost six months old. He loved to play with Robin's other dogs and "we just let him grow up and develop and have fun." At the age of six months, Robin started to show Bear. He was an instant winner. Right off the bat he took four first places in sanctioned matches in the area, and two first-place blue ribbons in point shows. (Sanctioned matches are matches sanctioned by the American Kennel Club but with no points awarded toward championship.) "I think his expression is what got him a long way in the ring," Robin said. "When you start looking at a dog you start at the head and try to get a balanced overall picture of the dog. Bear's best feature was always his head; I think a lot of the judges never got past his head."

It was then that Bear's eyes started tearing quite noticeably. Robin immediately took him to her vet who felt that Bear might have a touch of entropion, a condition that is sometimes caused by a muscle spasm within the eyelid. The eyelid rolls in, and the eyelashes and lid hairs hit the eye, causing constant irritations. Sometimes these irritations are only temporary and an eye ointment will clear them up. But sometimes the condition is hereditary. If that was the case with Bear, he would need a corrective eye operation, which, unfortunately, would eliminate him from the show ring. He

At six months, Bear won six first place ribbons in matches and shows.

would also have to be neutered to eliminate the possibility of passing the condition on to any offspring. An inherited condition would most certainly be the end of Robin's hopes for Bear as a champion show dog and foundation for breeding stock.

Robin's vet gave her an eye ointment to use on Bear to try and soothe the irritations, but it didn't seem to help. So Robin took Bear to Cornell University where he underwent a series of tests with eye specialists and, finally, a five-week, diagnostic nerve block to prevent his eyes from blinking. If the tearing were simply a result of irritations that weren't healing, the five-week block would give them time to rest and heal. But if Bear's eyes started tearing again after the block wore off, then the condition would most likely be hereditary and the corrective eye operation and the neutering would be necessary.

After almost five weeks to the day, Bear's eyes started to tear again. Robin was crushed. Everyone had come to love Bear so much. Robin spent several weeks trying to decide what to do. Then one day it occurred to a friend of hers, Pat Vogel, who is a 4-H Program Assistant for Dog Care and Training in the area, and who runs the area Puppy Raisers program with Guiding Eyes, to suggest to Robin, "What do you think about Bear as a guide dog?" Robin's immediate response was, "Do you think he could be?"

Pat called Jim Maginnis, the Breeding Farm Supervisor at Guiding Eyes, who was very impressed with Bear's bloodlines and background. Jim said that if Bear passed the Puppy Evaluation Testing and if Robin would keep him until he was a year old, then Guiding Eyes would take him. They would give Bear a couple of weeks of training. If he showed good potential, Guiding Eyes would have the eyelid surgery performed and also have him neutered. Then Bear would be assigned training.

Barb Nichols, a Puppy Evaluator for Guiding Eyes, tested Bear the next time she was in the area. The test involved firing a gun (blank) near Bear, opening an umbrella suddenly, and dropping a heavy metal chair, as well as a complete physical evaluation and testing of Bear in traffic for pace and consistency. Barb was impressed with Bear; he was "like a rock." She would come back for him in October when he was a year old.

Bear always loved to get in a car or truck and be off somewhere. "But," Robin told us, "that Monday afternoon in October was the first time he didn't want to get in." Robin's mother and sister, who had come along to give Robin moral support, disappeared, and so Barb pulled the front end and Robin pushed the back end. They got him into the van and put him in a crate. Robin remembered that Bear loves to chew and put a chew bone in along with him.

Robin waited and waited and waited. Then all of a sudden in December Pat got a report from Guiding Eyes that Bear had done well in his first training, that he'd had the eye operation in late November, and that all was looking good. After the eyes healed, Bear would start formal training;

119

he would soon be ready for the right person to come along.

"For the last couple of months that's all I've been waiting to hear, that they'd found the right person for Bear," Robin said. "Then I got the letter and invitation to Puppy Raisers Day. Actually, as Area Director, Pat received word first and called me right away: 'Bear got a person! Bear got a person!' "

At 2:30 it was time for Robin to start the long drive home; she didn't want to go. Seeing the love and special bond between Tom and Bear had made this the most rewarding experience of Robin's life. "He's happy. I can tell he's happy. That's the most important thing. It really makes you wonder about running these other dogs around in a show ring, making them stand there and pose. I told a friend of mine, a nun, about Bear, and she said to me, 'Isn't it wonderful that Bear's purpose is to help somebody else instead of being a show-off in the ring.' " Now Robin has no doubts that "this is what Bear was born to do." As Robin and her friend left, they promised to keep in touch with Tom and Bear.

Bear was born far away in Alaska a few months after Tom finally went blind. Problems with his eyes led Bear to Guiding Eyes, just as they had led Tom. Bear was being trained at Guiding Eyes while Tom was being trained at the Commission. Three weeks ago they met at Guiding Eyes for the first time. And now they are "Tom and Bear."

SUNDAY, JUNE 29, YORKTOWN HEIGHTS

Seeing green

MORNING. It was a rainy, dreary morning, in sharp contrast to yesterday. The airport limousine came for the students who were leaving early before most of us were up. We missed their voices at the breakfast table. I think everyone was thinking about home with mixed emotions. For the most part, the students have all really enjoyed each other and have become very close. It's hard to start saying good-bye. And Guiding Eyes itself has been a very warm and supportive place; everyone here is on the students' side. But the real world out there isn't always like that; there are lots of silent questions in everyone's mind about how it will be out there. On the other hand, home, as always, is simply home, and that's where everyone wants to be.

Billy told us he had been depressed yesterday. His wife had called in the late afternoon to say that her guide dog had died, a very sad and difficult moment for her. Billy thinks she will be back at Guiding Eyes in the spring for another dog. And he teased Don and Brenda about the possibility of having to put up with another Southerner.

After breakfast, Tom and Bear and Dan and Tucker all went to church. According to Tom, Bear managed a couple of fairly loud sighs during the sermon. Then Don took Tom and Bear on a country walk that was more like Tom's home area, where the houses are closer together and without side-walks or curbs. Bear worked well, and it relieved Tom's mind about home.

AFTERNOON. For Tom, going home means going back to Columbia, South Carolina, and his family. He'll practice working with Bear around home and around Columbia for the next couple of months and then go to the Commission for training on the Optacon this fall. The Optacon is a visual scanning device that transforms print in letters or books into letters that can actually be felt on the finger. The ability to use the Optacon is a prerequisite for a special training program Tom wants to take next year.

Tom plans to take a ten-month technical training course for the blind in computer programming. He'd like to finish college, but that would take at least three more years, if not longer. And he's anxious to be independent. Within a year he can complete the computer training program and have the skills to enter a field in which there are good jobs available, a field with a future. He's always loved mathematics, so he figures he's got to like computers.

Tom often experiences an interesting phenomenon. Although he's totally blind, he sees colors. They are not light perceptions, they are tricks of the brain. The doctors say it will eventually go away. I asked Tom what colors he had been seeing while we were talking about the future. Tom said, "Green. That's my favorite color." He was quiet for a moment and then said, "A little while ago I asked my priest what all the different colors stood for in the church. He said that green stands for hope. That made me feel good."

MONDAY, JUNE 30

Trains and exit interviews

MORNING. Most of the remaining students, with the exception of Tom and Dan, who stayed behind for their "exit interviews" with Geoff Lock, learned to work the platforms and trains of the nearby Croton-Harmon railroad station. Caroline worked Buffy with the Sonicguide. He seems to pick up speed and Caroline wonders if perhaps, with his sensitive ears, he's hearing the ultrasound. Using the Sonicguide with Buffy is still something of a question mark in Caroline's mind.

Geoff asked Tom, as he does each student at an exit interview, for his comments on the training, the facilities, and the services at Guiding Eyes. Geoff then went over Brenda's final report on Tom. Geoff reminded Tom that he is still expecting too much from Bear at times. He's expecting Bear to be perfect. Like all the other dogs, Bear has a tendency

Caroline, using the Sonicguide, and Buffy maneuver the long stairway at the Croton-Harmon railroad station.

to goof off now and then, and Tom is not as aware of it as he should be. Geoff reminded Tom that Bear tends to be a worrier and that he needs plenty of praise to build his confidence. And finally, Tom is using the "Hup-up" command too often; too many "Hup-ups" tend to confuse Bear and he starts worrying. Geoff congratulated Tom on his and Bear's work together.

AFTERNOON. The students were given the general layout of the Yorktown Heights shopping mall and encouraged to shop on their own or in pairs for an hour. At one point,

Bear led Tom, Dan, and Tucker into a ladies' fitting room, which caused a bit of commotion and then a good laugh.

Tucker has been wonderfully good for Dan; Tucker's taken Dan's mind off the fact that he's daily losing what little sight he has left. It's been hard for Dan. He's a proud man and he doesn't feel like a rock anymore. Like Tom, Dan lay around in bed for many months shutting himself off, listening to silence. Sharon says she can understand how Dan feels. "Dan's been seeing all his life, and all of a sudden not being able to see is really frightening. I think it was sort of good for me that I lost my sight when I was a little girl. It didn't bother me that much." Sharon thinks that having Tucker and being with other blind people at Guiding Eyes, "seeing how we all talk and laugh and play like everyone else," have helped bring Dan out of his shell a little. "In time, he will learn that it's not the end of the world."

Dan and Tucker.

TUESDAY, JULY 1, PEEKSKILL

The last day

MORNING AND AFTERNOON. A last day of free-lancing in Peekskill. Tom worked Bear several times through a narrow sidewalk area with overhanging shrubs. Bear still worries in these narrow situations, but they're working it out. The praise helps.

Caroline tried lowering the volume on the Sonicguide. Buffy kept a better pace and Caroline was able to avoid crowding him. Now it looks to Caroline as if it is going to work out fine. Marty, an Orientation and Mobility Specialist as well as Coordinator of Student Admissions, plugged an

Marty monitors Caroline's Sonicguide, hearing just what Caroline hears.

Overhanging obstacles such as tree branches can be difficult for some dogs; they see the world from a point of view much lower to the ground than we do.

earphone monitor into Caroline's Sonicguide during the walk so that he could hear the signals Caroline was picking up. Marty will visit Caroline and Buffy in Albany in a few weeks to check on how they're working. Guiding Eyes is very interested in exploring the use of the new electronic travel aids that are being developed for the blind and learning in detail how they affect guide dog work and training.

EVENING. Hectic. The van will take all the students to the airport at 5:00 A.M. tomorrow morning. There is much packing and exchanging of addresses. One last game of Hi Rollers. And one last game, and one last game, and one last game.

WEDNESDAY, JULY 2, YORKTOWN HEIGHTS

The last hours

5:00 A.M. Everything happened so quickly. It seemed like one moment the rooms were full of people and dogs and suitcases and noise, and in the next the van had pulled away and everyone was gone. The emptiness was so abrupt and the silence overwhelming. It was an eerie feeling walking back to my room, slowly shutting the lights off one by one. I felt like yelling at the top of my lungs, "Where are you all?"

I closed the door of my room. It was still dark, so I stretched out on the bed and lay very still. Faintly at first, I heard a morning bird begin to sing. And then another, and another, beginning the new day. As the sky slowly lightened, I realized that it was, indeed, a new day.

Caroline awakened me at 8:00 to say good-bye; Marty was taking her to the Croton-Harmon station where she and Buffy would catch the train for Albany. Another hug, and

Geoff Lock, Director of Guiding Eyes.

another good-bye. I got some coffee from the kitchen and sat out under the Norway spruce.

As Geoff crossed the lawn, he saw me and invited me to ride over to the site of the new breeding farm, where guide dog work literally begins, with him and Jim Maginnis. It was only a few weeks away from being ready now, a beautiful modern facility overlooking a pond. As Geoff drove, we talked a bit about the class. This was a strong class, and all of the students should do well at home.

Above: the new breeding farm is across the pond and beyond the great oak. Below: the kennel and runs are not quite finished.

Once in a while, a student returns a dog after a few months because the dog isn't working well or isn't adjusting well. Sometimes that's actually true, but more often than not it is the student who has decided that he or she doesn't want the responsibility of a dog and uses the dog as an excuse. That's okay. A student who doesn't genuinely want the responsibility of a dog shouldn't have one. If a dog is returned, it is either retrained and reassigned or Guiding Eyes finds it a good home.

When a dog gets too old to work, usually after eight to ten years, the student can retire the dog and keep it at home, or return the dog to Guiding Eyes. If the dog is not too sick or infirm, Guiding Eyes finds it a home for its last years. Most students who are able to, keep the dogs. "But," Geoff says, "some of them are able to trade in a dog for a new model like you and I trade in cars."

When we returned, I stopped in to see Ted Zubrycki, Director of Training, to thank him for his patience and his many insights into guide dog training and work. Ted is a little worried about Tom and Bear. Bear needs constant praise and confidence building, support under stress. It will take time.

Don and Brenda and Bill, who have just about lived with the class twenty-four hours a day, will have a few days off and then begin training a new string of dogs. Charlie admitted, now that it was all over, that he had been really nervous about the days in White Plains.

My ride back to New York picked me up about 3:00 P.M. It will be good to get home. But like the students, part of me will stay behind.

Tom's Journal

THE FIRST DAYS AT HOME

WEDNESDAY, JULY 2. The trip from Guiding Eyes to the airport didn't take long. I didn't realize until I was finally leaving the place how much I would miss it.

There's one advantage to being blind: we were the first ones on the plane. All the stewardesses loved Bear and all the people around me started talking about dogs. The lady behind me said Bear and I looked like newlyweds.

Now that I have a dog instead of a cane, it all seems so different. People come up and just start talking to me.

When Bear first saw the family, he was kind of nervous and scared. He didn't want to see anyone at first, he wanted to hide. So he put his head between my legs. After a minute he went up to them one by one, wagging his tail, licking them, being himself again.

When our other dog saw me and Bear get out of the car, he growled and barked. He was really mad.

I took Bear around to the rooms one by one on the leash, but we spent most of the time in my bedroom. He parked okay but he didn't eat much.

THURSDAY, JULY 3. It was still kind of dark at 6:00 this morning when my dad looked in to wake me up. Bear growled at him. Makes me feel good that Bear is looking out for me.

He only ate a handful this morning. I kept him on the leash and took him around to all the rooms again. And I walked him around outside and introduced him to our other

Back home in Columbia, South Carolina, Tom and Bear set out to explore the neighborhood.

dog. Bear sniffed and wagged his tail. But he went crazy when he saw our duck. Must have reminded him of his retriever instincts. I don't think he would have harmed the duck. He just likes to play; he still has a lot of puppy in him.

FRIDAY, JULY 4. Had Dad wake me at 6:30 this morning. Bear growled again. I let him loose around the house and

In August, Tom and Bear visited New York where they explored a special exhibition of sculpture at New York University's Grey Gallery. Tom tried to feel and sense the body position of a Rodin sculpture, and Bear tried to figure out what Tom was doing.

At the Dutchess County Fair, Tom and Bear had an opportunity to see a 4-H calf up close. Bear declined.

he loved looking in all the rooms and sniffing in all the corners. He picked up anything that looked like a shoe or slipper and brought it to me. And he picked up a lot of my little brother Ronald's toys and brought them too. Now maybe Ronald will learn to pick them up! Still not eating much.

SATURDAY, JULY 5. It was too hot to work Bear during the day so I let him roam around the house more freely. We went to 5:00 mass this evening. Bear did perfectly with the doors and the curbs. We sat in the back and Bear lay down under the pew.

In the evening I heeled him around the block with my dad following behind. I showed Bear all the places he should stop. And Bear saw all the neighborhood and street dogs.

THURSDAY, JULY 10. Bear's eating fine now. He went after a puppy in our driveway, wanted to play. I corrected him. Then he started to veer out toward the middle of the road where some other dogs were. I corrected him for that too. I was going to bop his nose, but he saw my hand coming toward him and knew he was goofing off. He moved right back to the left and stayed there.

FRIDAY, JULY 11. We worked the four blocks again without a mistake. I'm really proud of Bear today. I'm always proud of him, but especially today. He completely ignored all the other dogs and distractions. We'll try some different variations of the route now.

At night, before we go to bed, Bear checks around all the rooms to see if everyone is okay and tells everyone good night.

Photos on pages 135–39 courtesy of Sterling Steffensen

Back Home

I've been in touch with all of the students to see how they're doing back home, and because they are all friends now. Like Tom, they've all had some problems to work out, new experiences to work through.

HOWARD AND MARTY. Marty does real well at the plant. The noise from the machines doesn't seem to bother him at all, except for a loud vacuum cleaner. Everyone at work loves Marty and one of the ladies even brought a rug for me to put under my table for him. Marty is very lovable.

EILEEN AND INDY. My sister and dad came to meet us at the airport. As I worked Indy off the plane, they had their backs turned, looking the other way. Indy walked

Howard and Marty

Eileen and Indy

135

straight over to my dad. I don't know if he had a special scent about him or not, but we have a joke about it now: "the Abbott family scent."

One day on the bus I heard a lady tell another that Indy was also "a trained guard dog." There are a lot of misconceptions about that. But that's okay too.

I took Indy to the lake with me; she loves to hike and swim. Indy is a good co-worker and a good companion. I don't think I'd ever be without a dog again.

JOE AND TOBIAS. Tobias has adjusted very well and is the hit of the neighborhood. People love to pet him. I'm going to have to be more strict about that.

Tobias' 4-H family sent my wife JoAnn some pictures from Puppy Raisers Day. JoAnn should be delivering our first child just about the time you are all up at the Walk-A-Thon this fall.

SHARON AND NOLAN. In the beginning having a dog is very frustrating. Nolan is curious about everything, has to stop ten times to smell. I keep correcting him and people keep telling me that I'm being "mean to the dog." Like they

Joe and Tobias

Sharon and Nolan

said at Guiding Eyes, you really can't pay attention to what people think, as long as *you* know what you're doing.

Everyone at school loves Nolan and brings him cookies and bones all the time. Everyone comes to see Nolan and I start to think, "But what about me?" He should love it here.

Nolan makes me laugh so much.

BILLY AND DOLLY. The family is really crazy about Dolly; so am I. She learned our route to work real well and we walk her two miles a day when we take our little girl to the park. Two miles in fifteen minutes! That's pretty good! Dolly just hightails it down the street.

As I was getting off the bus the other day, I picked up Dolly's handle for balance, like you're supposed to, and I overheard one lady say to another, "Why, look at that nice man. He's leading that poor old blind dog around. Bless his heart." That kind of makes you stop and think.

ANITA AND SUE. Sue and the children get along fine. The littlest, Angela, crawls right over to her and plays with her. Christina was afraid at first, but after three days fell in

Billy and Dolly

Anita and Sue

love with her and can't keep away from her now. I have to keep reminding them that Sue is my dog.

Sue has created some problems. She's still very exuberant and overly friendly with other people and other dogs. She's easily distracted. She works pretty well, but tends to overrun intersections; we don't have many sidewalks and curbs around here.

ROSS AND LANCE. I'm still disappointed that I didn't get a shepherd, but I'm satisfied with Lance. He's a real good-natured dog and he's learning the campus at school pretty well. He's adapting.

BOB AND RAFT. Raft and I have been taking it easy this summer, getting ready for Boston College this fall. I'm a lot more independent with Raft; we go all over the place. He hates to be left alone. When I leave him alone he gets into a wastebasket and pulls everything out. I gave him a bath and he was great . . . just stood there.

JOYCE AND OWEN. When I first got home, Owen and my little boy, Sean, were quite jealous of each other. It's

Ross and Lance

Bob and Raft

Joyce and Owen

funny the way they try to outdo each other. It's nice to feel so wanted.

I'm pretty restricted now. When Sean goes to school in the fall, I should be able to get out more. But I'm worried about using the bus and I'm waiting for an instructor to come out and help me with buses and trains.

Life seems a little dull after Guiding Eyes.

DAN AND TUCKER. I'm getting out a little more now. Tucker takes me about ten blocks every morning to early mass and he always does perfect. I have a special ground hook for him out in the backyard so he can exercise and play. Tucker is really changing my life.

CAROLINE AND BUFFY. Buffy is a little hesitant about doing new things; it takes a lot of encouragement. But he's adjusted well now to the Sonicguide and is much more alert without Don and Brenda and Charlie around. But all the things they ever said keep coming back to me. All the learning is coming together for us now.

I'd forgotten about how much care a dog takes. But if you love the beast, you don't mind.

Dan and Tucker

Caroline and Buffy

Sixth Annual Walk-A-Thon

During its twenty-five-year history, Guiding Eyes for the Blind, Inc., has provided over 2,300 guide dogs and training to blind people from all over the country and from around the world. On October 12, Tom and Bear, Dan and Tucker, Eileen and Indy, Howard and Marty, along with more than sixty other former students and their dogs, and many friends and supporters of Guiding Eyes from surrounding communities, gathered at Mohansic State Park for Guiding Eyes' Sixth Annual Walk-A-Thon. The purpose of the Walk-A-Thon, a ten-mile walk around the park—fifteen for sighted volunteers—is to raise money for future programs and training and thereby offer more blind people the opportunity of greater freedom and independence.

Assisting a Guide Dog Team

From my days at Guiding Eyes, I learned that blind people know a great deal more about where they are and what they are doing than I had realized. They focus their hearing and other senses in the way that we focus our sight. And often they are paying more attention. They have to. But everyone needs some assistance once in a while. Here are a few things to remember:

Ask first. Never just grab a blind person. No matter how it may look to you, assistance may not be needed. More than once I've seen a blind team at a corner, aligning for a turn, suddenly grabbed and whisked across a street they hadn't been trying to cross. It's very disorienting.

Let the blind person take your left arm. And give them time to drop the harness handle and "heel" the dog.

Be patient. Stop for all curbs and stairs. Give the blind person time to locate the curb or step with his or her left foot. The dog must stop and sit at each curb and step when "heeling", and then must be praised.

Before leaving, help orient the blind person to his or her new location. Be sure the blind person knows exactly where he or she is and is facing in a straight direction forward.

Don't shout phrases like "watch out!" or "the light's green." The blind person doesn't know what to watch out for and doesn't know how long the light has been green; he or she may not have time to cross safely. In fact, there's no need to shout at all. It's amazing how many people think blind people are hard of hearing.

If you want to ask a blind person about his or her dog, step up, introduce yourself, and ask. Most blind people are happy to talk about their dogs, but don't enjoy hearing people whisper about them behind their backs.

And don't be offended if a blind person refuses your assistance. Being independent is an important goal for all guide dog teams. Achieving it, as so many do, deserves our admiration and praise. Instead of being insulted, tell them—and mean it—"You're terrific!" It's true.

Guide Dog Schools

These guide dog schools are listed by the American Foundation for the Blind, Inc. in their "Directory of Agencies Serving the Visually Handicapped in the United States" and are of long-standing reputation.

New York:
    Guiding Eyes for the Blind, Inc.
    611 Granite Springs Road
    Yorktown Heights, New York 10598

    Guide Dog Foundation for the Blind, Inc.
    109–19 72nd Avenue
    Forest Hills, New York 11375

New Jersey:
    The Seeing Eye, Inc.
    P.O. Box 375
    Morristown, New Jersey 07960

Ohio:
    Pilot Dogs, Inc.
    625 West Town Street
    Columbus, Ohio 43215

Michigan:
Leader Dogs for the Blind
1039 Rochester Road
Rochester, Michigan 48063

California:
Guide Dogs for the Blind, Inc.
P.O. Box 1200
San Rafael, California 94902

International Guiding Eyes, Inc.
5431 Denny Avenue
North Hollywood, California 91603

Hawaii:
Eye of the Pacific Guide Dogs, Inc.
3008 Kalei Road
Honolulu, Hawaii 96814

Glossary

bedchain a short chain, approximately two feet in length, one end of which attaches to a dog's collar and the other end to the leg of a bed or a wall hook to restrict a dog to a small area.

blood sugar sugar, in the form of glucose, that has been absorbed into the bloodstream.

choke chain a metal-link dog collar, used in the training of mature dogs, which tightens around the neck when pulled or jerked and eases when the tension on it is relaxed.

corneal dysplasia the abnormal growth or development of the cornea, the tough, transparent outer covering of the eye that admits light to the interior.

correction a reprimand to a guide dog in the form of the vocal command, "No!" or a sudden, sharp jerk on the leash for either poor behavior or an incorrect action.

cystic fibrosis a hereditary, glandular disorder that usually appears in early childhood, characterized by respiratory symptoms and the excessive loss of salt.

diabetes a disease in which sugar and starch are not properly absorbed by the body, characterized by excessive urine secretion.

diabetic retinopathy the degeneration of the retina due to diabetes.

downcurb a curb which requires a step down, such as from the sidewalk to the street.

entropion a turning inward of the eyelid.

glaucoma a disease of the eye marked by increased pressure of the fluid within the eyeball, causing weakening or loss of sight.

glucose the simplest form of sugar; the form of sugar by which carbohydrates are absorbed by the body.

heartworm a principally canine parasite, spread by mosquitoes in the form of microscopic larvae which enter an infected animal's bloodstream, mature, and eventually lodge in the heart and lungs.

"heel" a command used in obedience training and guide dog work, requiring a dog to walk on the left side of his master, keeping his shoulders close to his master's left knee at all times and his head facing straight to the front.

"hup-up" a command used in guide dog work to tell the dog one of three things: (1) pick up the pace; (2) pay attention and get back to work; or (3) move a little closer to a curb or obstacle.

insulin a protein hormone produced in the pancreas, regulating the absorption of sugar by the body.

intelligent disobedience the refusal on the part of a guide dog to obey a command that the dog sees or perceives to be unsafe.

nerve block an injection of a local anesthesia that causes a temporary paralysis of a muscle or a loss of sensation in the area.

Optacon a visual scanning device used by the blind or visually impaired that transforms print so that it can actually be felt on the fingertips.

ophthalmologist a physician, an M.D., who specializes in the diagnosis and treatment of defects and diseases of the eye, performing surgery when necessary.

optometrist a licensed, nonmedical practitioner, who measures irregularities in the size or shape of the eyeball or surface of the cornea and eye muscle disturbances. Treatment is limited to glasses, prisms, and exercises.

peripheral vision the ability to perceive the presence, motion, or color of objects outside the direct line of vision.

point show a dog show, licensed by the American Kennel Club, in which points are awarded toward championship.

retina a layer of membrane at the back of the eyeball sensitive to light and connected to the optic nerve.

retinitis pigmentosa an hereditary degeneration or atrophy of the retina.

retinoblastoma a malignant tumor within the eyeball that usually occurs in children under 5 and is present most often at birth.

retrain a blind person who has previously been trained with a guide dog and who is currently undergoing retraining with a new dog.

sanctioned match a dog show, approved by the American Kennel Club, but with no points awarded toward championship.

sighted-guide any person who serves as a guide for the blind.

Sonicguide an electronic travel aid used by the blind or visually impaired in conjunction with a cane or guide dog.

upcurb a curb which requires a step up, such as from the street to the sidewalk.